The Way to Ware

Scala/paſſuum

80 160 240 320 400 480

ore feyldes

Spittle feyldes

Buſhopes gate

S. Botolph

Aldgate

towne

Poſterne

East Smithfeyld

The ſtiliarde

Shreweſburye houſe

Olde ſwann

Lion kaye

Bellyns gate

Custom howſe

Galley kaye

The towre

S. Katherynes

fluuius

S. Marye Oueryes

20

S. Towleyes

LONDON
1000 YEARS

LONDON

1000 YEARS

TREASURES FROM THE COLLECTIONS
OF THE CITY OF LONDON

Edited by David Pearson

ACKNOWLEDGMENTS

Many of the items in this book are held on deposit by the City of London Corporation on behalf of organisations and individuals, so as to ensure their safe custody while making them available for the public. Permission to reproduce the images has always been sought where appropriate, and we are grateful for all the agreements that were given. We are also happy to acknowledge with thanks the following specific permissions, as requested by the owners: the Dean and Chapter of St Paul's Cathedral, London (pp. 34, 129); Royal Sun Alliance (p. 61); the Trustees of Guy's and St Thomas's Charity (p. 70); the Worshipful Company of Parish Clerks (p. 73); the Thomas Coram Foundation for Children (Coram) (pp. 74–75); the Spanish and Portuguese Jews Congregation of London (p. 83); Thames Water Utilities Ltd (p. 111).

All the staff who have contributed text to this book (see p. 160) were involved in the selection of material and in the shaping of the finished product, and their efforts are much appreciated. The editor would also like to thank Rosalina Banfield, his assistant, for helping to co-ordinate the work, and Esme West, at Scala, for keeping the project on the straight and narrow. Nick Bodger helped with proofreading. The photography for the book was undertaken by the Image & Media staff at London Metropolitan Archives, and it could not have been produced without the work of Doug Bartram-Weight and his colleagues, to whom many thanks are also due.

The support of the City of London Corporation to the work involved in producing this book is gratefully acknowledged.

Abbreviations used in citations/references

GAG   Guildhall Art Gallery
GHL   Guildhall Library
KH   Keats House
LMA   London Metropolitan Archives

Endpapers:
John Norden, Map of the City
of London (detail)
Engraving on paper, 1593
LMA Pr.Gp.1

Half-title:
Transcripts of charters and statutes,
1 Edward III to 11 Henry VII
Manuscript on vellum, 1327–1495,
detail of fol. 134v
LMA COL/CS/01/007

Title page:
Richard Paton and Francis Wheatley,
*The Lord Mayor's Procession by Water
to Westminster, November 9th 1789*
Oil on canvas, 1789–92
GAG 54

◀◀ **The Pearl Sword**
Various metals with fabric and
pearls, 16th century
Mansion House Plate Collection

◀ **The State Sword**
Various metals and fabric,
17th century
Mansion House Plate Collection

CONTENTS

▶ John White, Mace of the
City of London Corporation
Silver-gilt, 1735
Mansion House Plate Collection

LORD MAYOR'S FOREWORD

s the 684th Lord Mayor of the City of London, I know that the City has a long history. The first of my predecessors that we can identify, Henry Fitz-Ailwin, took up office in 1189, but we know that before him there were other individuals and groups of citizens leading the affairs of London. The unbroken line of 683 Lord Mayors before me reflects the stability of the City as a focal point in the affairs of London and the nation, a centre of trade, politics and influence over many centuries.

In the course of that history the City of London Corporation has come to look after collections of outstanding importance that reflect life, art and how we come to be where we are today. The City Corporation's own archives stretch back to the Norman Conquest and constitute an important part of the national record. Its books and paintings, complemented by a wealth of other material in its care, have established it as a major centre for curating or discovering the history of London. This book is all about celebrating and showcasing those collections, and I am delighted to be able to welcome it and commend it.

History, and its manifestations, are important to us. History helps us to understand where we have come from, it gives us roots, and it teaches us lessons about human behaviour. Our collections are used by people of all ages as sources of learning as well as of wonderment, and in this digital age they are increasingly being made accessible to the world through the potential of digitisation and the internet. The City has always been a forward-looking place, and it is important to open up and interpret our history as well as to safeguard it. This book should enhance the appreciation not only of these outstanding resources but also of the role the City Corporation plays in preserving, and promoting, such an important part of our total national heritage.

David Wootton
Lord Mayor of the City of London

◄ **The Fire Cup**
Silver gilt, originally made in
1580, reworked in 1662
Mansion House Plate Collection

▲ **'SS collar'**
Gold, enamel and diamonds,
16th century
Mansion House Plate Collection

INTRODUCTION

◀ Dante Gabriel Rossetti,
La Ghirlandata (detail)
Oil on canvas, 1873
GAG 1059
(see p. 150)

'The City of London' is a phrase with multiple meanings. In the broadest sense, it may be used to mean the whole conurbation of inner and outer London, the nation's capital city, with its 1,572 square kilometres and 7.7 million inhabitants. More correctly, it may refer to the geographical area sometimes known as the 'Square Mile', once bounded by a medieval wall, which is the historic centre of habitation and trade from which the rest of London grew. It runs, roughly, from Chancery Lane to the Tower of London (west to east) and from Moorgate to the Thames (north to south). The words may also be used as a synonym for the business that most famously goes on there; this district – housing the Bank of England, the Stock Exchange and numerous banking and insurance headquarters – is one of the world's key hubs for financial services. 'He works in the City' usually points to someone employed in one of these powerhouses of monetary affairs, not just in that defined geographical area but also more widely across London. The word is also used as shorthand for the City of London Corporation, the administrative body that governs the activities of the Square Mile, and it is in this sense that 'the City' is a key presence throughout this book.

The City Corporation has many functions. As a legal entity, with responsibilities to regulate public life, it is older than Parliament. Its incorporation is regarded as having happened by prescription, since time immemorial, before written documentation could confirm it. Its governance model, with a Lord Mayor, aldermen and a Court of Common Council, evolved during the Middle Ages and has remained in place ever since. Today it provides local-government-type services for the Square Mile, but it undertakes a range of activities beyond those normally run from town halls: it runs important recreational facilities outside its boundaries (such as Epping Forest and Hampstead Heath), it has its own police force, and it is the principal funder of an internationally renowned arts centre (the Barbican). The Corporation's historic development has brought it endowments that allow it to exercise these wider responsibilities for public benefit. In recent years it has also become a major advocate for the importance of the Square Mile as a business district, and the Lord Mayor now spends a significant part of his time acting as an international ambassador for the United Kingdom's trade and investment.

The City Corporation is also the custodian of a significant part of the nation's, and particularly London's, heritage. Its own records run back in almost continuous sequence to the time of the Norman Conquest, and it has over the centuries acquired major collections of books, documents, paintings, prints, photographs, maps, ephemera and more relating to London's history. Ever since Guildhall Library opened as a public facility in the nineteenth century, the City's libraries and archives have drawn to them a huge wealth of material given or deposited by others, who have understood the benefits to be had from a critical mass of related resources. The collections have therefore come to be a major centre for all aspects of the history of London, from all periods and extending far beyond the Square Mile. The purpose of this book is to showcase these collections, and to raise awareness of the amazing range of material that can be found there.

The archive holdings now unified at London Metropolitan Archives bring together three significant but related collections: the City Corporation's own archives (held before 2005 in what was called the Corporation of London Records Office), the manuscript collections of Guildhall Library (including the deposited archives of numerous City parishes, livery companies and businesses) and the contents of what used to be the Greater London Record Office (before the abolition of the Greater London Council in 1986). This includes a great quantity of material documenting the running of London more widely, embracing courts, schools, hospitals, charities, urban planning and more. In all, these collections occupy about 90 kilometres of shelving, and they create one of the most extensive municipal archive centres in the world today.

The Corporation's own archives inevitably include much material relating to national as well as local affairs. Before the expansion of London from the eighteenth century onwards, the City effectively spoke for the population and commerce of the whole of the capital and was a major player on the constitutional stage. The dynamics changed as the metropolis grew, and the Greater London Record Office collections tell the story of the various bodies set up to govern London more widely, including the many boards and subsidiaries of the London County Council (established in 1889 and replaced by the Greater London Council in 1965). The Greater London Authority (the most recent incarnation of pan-London administration, set up in 2000) continues the tradition of depositing its archival records with the City. Many of these wider London collections have an extensive historical reach; the Middlesex Sessions of the Peace cover the administrative and judicial affairs of metropolitan London from the sixteenth century onwards.

Guildhall Library traces its roots to a medieval foundation which has sometimes been called England's first public library. This is a good strapline, if something of an over-simplification, but recent research has shown that the fifteenth-century Guildhall Library was indeed the earliest library in England to be freely available to anyone who wished to use it, although geared primarily to the needs of local clergymen. This first library was established as one of the benefactions from the estate of Richard (Dick) Whittington in the 1420s and was built adjoining the Guildhall. It continued to operate for a century and more, supported by a number of gifts and further bequests, but was plundered in its entirety in 1549 (see p. 27), and today we have only a small handful of surviving books.

The library as we know it today dates back to 1824, when a new collection of mostly printed material on London and Middlesex began to be built up, for the use of the Corporation. This quickly grew and was opened as a public reference library, in a handsome purpose-built reading room adjacent to the Guildhall, in 1872. It has been a key component of the Guildhall complex of buildings ever since but moved to the other side of Guildhall Yard in 1974, into the new west-wing block which replaced a late eighteenth-century range of buildings.

Although Guildhall Library is equipped to help with reference enquiries across many subjects, its particular strengths are around the history of London, where its printed collections are both comprehensive and internationally recognised. It holds around 50,000 books printed before 1851, with extensive coverage of rare imprints relating to London, and its sets of poll books and London trade directories rival those of the British Library. It has a number of special collections, including those focused on Sir Thomas More (see p. 133) and John Wilkes (see p. 38); it also has important holdings around City trades and the development of commerce in the City.

The City Corporation began to acquire paintings in the late seventeenth century (see p. 137), and has since accumulated a collection of around 4,000 oils and watercolours. These include many scenes of London, as well as depictions of City ceremonial, and also some spectacular highlights, such as the collection of Pre-Raphaelite and other Victorian paintings bequeathed by Charles Gassiot (p. 150), the Samuel

Collection of Dutch Masters (p. 139) and the studio collection of Sir Matthew Smith (p. 153). A gallery for the display of the collection was first erected at the side of Guildhall Yard in 1886, and the Corporation has been committed to public access to the paintings ever since. The original gallery was destroyed by bombing in 1940 (the pictures having been moved to safe storage), and a rather sub-standard replacement post-war building lasted until 1987, when it was demolished to make way for the handsome gallery we know today, which opened in 1999. The paintings complement the huge range of other graphic items found elsewhere across the collections, including over 250,000 prints, etchings and watercolours, and over 300,000 photographs of London. The archives also house a growing collection of films from the early twentieth century onwards.

The focus of this book is on printed, written, photographed, drawn or painted materials, but it should be added that heritage is manifested in the City Corporation in other important ways too. Its buildings comprise an important part of the historical geography of the Square Mile. The Guildhall and its Great Hall have constituted the administrative and symbolic centre of the City for many centuries, not only as the place where those in charge of the City's affairs meet in council but also as a place of trials, ceremonies and entertainments. The Guildhall as we know it today began to be built in 1411, so this book is published in the year of its 600th anniversary, but there are references to a meeting hall here at least as far back as the early twelfth century. Guildhall Yard, by which the Great Hall is approached, commemorates an even

older structure, as its floor tiles include a large ellipse marking out the walls of the Roman amphitheatre that was built here around AD 120. Remains of the amphitheatre were discovered when Guildhall Art Gallery was reconstructed in the 1990s and can now be visited whenever the gallery is open. Little now remains of Roman London, but traces such as this remind us that the Square Mile was the site of Roman Londinium from the first century onwards, and that it was the original area of human settlement from which the rest of London grew.

The story of London as seen through objects and artefacts is told most obviously in the Museum of London, which is part-funded by the City Corporation. The museum looks after the Lord Mayor's state coach, although it is displayed in Guildhall before each annual Lord Mayor's Show. Other noteworthy pieces of historic City regalia are preserved at Mansion House, the official residence of the Lord Mayor and itself another important piece of built heritage. Standing opposite the Bank of England, it was built between 1739 and 1752 in grand Palladian style. Its plate room houses important pieces of ceremonial metalwork, such as the City's silver-gilt mace, dating from 1735 (see p. 5), and the Pearl Sword (see p. 4), reputedly brought by Elizabeth I to the opening of the Royal Exchange in 1571. Its scabbard contains over 2,000 pearls, sewn on both sides. The gold 'SS collar' is an outstanding piece of Tudor jewellery, incorporating enamel and diamonds in solid gold (see p. 7), and was bequeathed by Lord Mayor Sir John Aleyn in 1535 for the use of his successors. The plate room also holds an extensive collection of gold and silver tableware from the eighteenth century onwards, but the only surviving example of earlier City plate

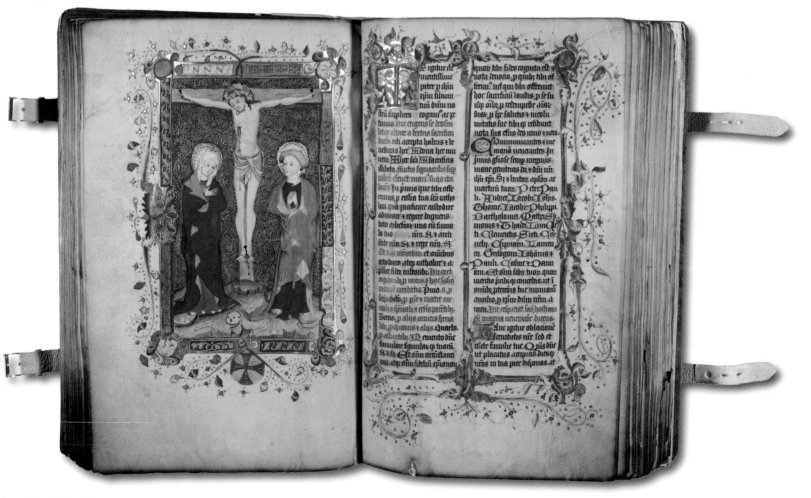

to have survived the Great Fire of 1666 is the covered chalice reworked in 1662, known as the Fire Cup (see p. 6).

The City Corporation's collections represent the documented memory of London over a thousand years and are a hugely important part of our cultural heritage. They were formally designated as being of national and international significance by the Museums, Libraries and Archives Council in 2005. Architects and surveyors come to use the files of London building plans, PhD students come to find new slants on medieval letter books, and schoolchildren come to have their history lessons brought alive by experiencing original materials. The many parochial, institutional and business registers comprise an essential quarry for family historians worldwide. Historical collections such as this tell stories at every level, from the micro to the macro, from the personal to the national, and this book's contents have been chosen to try to reflect that. It includes much that is spectacular and iconic, such as Magna Carta or the Shakespeare first folio, but also less high-profile objects that throw just as much light – if not more – on aspects of London life and represent rich seams of material to be discovered.

The items were selected and documented by expert staff who work with the collections, and the challenge was always to decide what could be left out rather than to find things to include. For everything that was chosen for inclusion to illustrate a particular theme there were numerous other equally interesting possibilities for which we did not have space. To put it another way, it is likely that everyone who knows these collections will open the book and declaim about the omission of favourite items. This merely emphasises, again, that point about the range of the material: the aim was to assemble a representative overview from across the whole, and what we have here is only a taster, to stimulate you to come and discover more. Further information about the collections and the services that make them accessible will be found on the City Corporation's website, and everyone is welcome – indeed encouraged – to explore further.

The City and Beyond

The City has been a hugely important agent in the history of the nation. Monarchs and governments over the centuries have been keen to engage with it, recognising the potential for influencing political and economic agendas that is exercised through the combination of people, wealth and trade concentrated in the Square Mile. Correspondingly, the City has been keen to play its role in national affairs and use its muscle in the interests of the rights and prosperity of its citizens. This relationship has been ongoing since at least 1066, when William the Conqueror understood the value of placating and accommodating the City, rather than trying to vanquish it, as is testified in the document shown opposite.

This chapter illustrates a variety of material from the collections that document the City Corporation's own development as a corporate organisation, and the role it has played in wider national and international affairs. It includes items that show how the administration emerged, including the roles of the Lord Mayor, aldermen and Common Council and the geographical wards. All of these aspects of City governance, which can be traced back to the Middle Ages, remain in place today and have helped to influence the ways in which other institutions have shaped themselves.

The City Corporation's archives are rich in medieval documents, from which only a few highlights can be selected here. The particularly fine 1297 issue of Magna Carta is an obvious treasure, but the 1215 mayoral charter shown with it is also a major milestone in the carving out of citizens' rights from those of the Crown (see pp. 16 and 17). It is one of a series of royal charters issued from the eleventh century onwards, defining or confirming the privileges of the City and those who live there. Some of the substantial illuminated legal compilations, such as the *Liber Horn* and *Cartae Antiquae*, are visually impressive but also reflect the growing solidity of the City's administrative machinery in the later medieval period. The letter books contain a huge wealth of historical information about London life at that time, supplemented by other sources such as the *Great Chronicle*, also shown here.

The City has always understood the importance of civic spectacle and ceremonial occasions, both for reasons of state and for the maintenance of popular morale, and many of its customs in this area have ancient roots. The annual Lord Mayor's Banquet, which is now addressed by the Prime Minister of the day, has been held in Guildhall since 1501 but can be traced back further still, to feasts held in livery halls. The Lord Mayor's Show also stretches back at least to the sixteenth century, and probably earlier, as an occasion for festivities and civic display. These events are variously represented in the collections, in pictures, in memorabilia produced in association with particular occasions and in account books that record how it was all organised and paid for. Examples are shown from the sixteenth century onwards of City pageants and banquets, seen through a number of lenses, including the eyes of artists, as well as the surviving documentation. Feasts and displays have always invited multiple interpretations, including the irreverent as well as the appreciative; the lampooning of perceived excess is nothing new, as seen from the work of Hogarth and the anonymous nineteenth-century cartoonist who imagined the nightmare of Lord Mayor John Key.

The role of the City Corporation in national affairs has changed over time. Its relationship with the Crown or the government of the day has often been a complex one, being both a part of the establishment and a force to be reckoned with in its own right. The disputes with medieval monarchs and the opposition to government policy over America in the eighteenth century (see p. 38) reflect in different ways, and many centuries apart, past tensions that have existed between Westminster and the City. The place of the City in modern life has been shaped by a series of changes and administrative reforms in London that began in the nineteenth century (see p. 126); today's Lord Mayor would no longer be a signatory to national treaties, or accompany the sovereign to quell rebellion, but continues to promote the good of both the nation and the Square Mile through international advocacy on behalf of the City's business interests. That is a principle that would have been recognised by Dick Whittington, and other medieval Lord Mayors.

▶ **Charter of William I to the City of London**
Manuscript on vellum, with seal, 1067
LMA COL/CH/01/001A

The City and the Conqueror

This small but iconic piece of vellum, the 'William Charter', is the oldest document in the City Corporation's archive, given by King William I (the Conqueror) to the City in 1067, soon after the Battle of Hastings but before he entered the City of London. It has been in the City's keeping ever since. It measures just 6 inches by 1½, with two slits, the larger one used as a seal-tongue and the other as a tie. The seal impression, although detached and imperfect, is one of the earliest surviving examples from William's reign.

It is written in Old English (and so, notably, not in William's native Norman French) and in the form of an administrative letter, a style commonly used by early English kings. Translated into modern English, it reads: 'William King greets William the Bishop and Geoffrey the Portreeve and all the citizens in London, French and English, in friendly fashion; and I inform you that it is my will that your laws and customs be preserved as they were in King Edward's day, that every son shall be his father's heir after his father's death; and that I will not that any man do wrong to you. God yield you.'

The charter reflects William's recognition of the importance of London, and of its concentration of trade and wealth, which he wished to safeguard. After defeating the English army under Harold at the Battle of Hastings in October 1066, William brought his forces on a slow and marauding march north, subjugating towns along the way, before forming an encampment at Westminster. He threatened to besiege and ransack the City, where many of the remaining leading men of the Anglo-Saxon court had congregated, and the subsequent peaceful surrender, for which the charter was a reward, was good for both sides. It was issued soon after William's coronation in Westminster Abbey on Christmas Day 1066, and was a key means whereby he won the support of Londoners; the degree of autonomy that it guaranteed has been valued and defended by the City ever since. The charter also reflects London's already established international character by addressing both the French and English residents and treating them with equal status.

It is especially significant not only for its survival but also because it is the earliest known royal or imperial document to guarantee the collective rights of the inhabitants of any town (it is not directed to specific groups, such as merchants, or to institutions, such as major churches). The charter granted nothing new to the Londoners but confirmed the citizens' rights and privileges already in existence. One of their primary concerns, as expressed in this charter, was to ensure that the succession to property was not subject to arbitrary royal intervention.

The document is one in a long line of charters that the citizens of London extracted from the sovereign; there are over a hundred royal charters in the City Corporation's archive. In 2010 the document was inscribed in the UNESCO United Kingdom Memory of the World Register, an online catalogue created to recognise documents of outstanding national cultural significance and to support and raise international awareness of archives and their importance. **ES**

Magna Carta and the City's liberties

The tribulations of King John, and his quarrels with his subjects, have become part of English historical folklore and are familiar to anyone who knows the story of Robin Hood. The concessions John had to make to maintain peace mean that his reign is often perceived as particularly important for the development of the English constitution and for the establishment of people's rights and liberties.

The charter on the left here is one of the milestones in the evolution of City government. John became king in 1199, but by 1215 he was faced with a major rebellion. Hoping to win the Londoners to his side, he granted them the right to choose annually a mayor, who should be faithful, discreet and fit for the government of the City. In doing this, he was confirming a custom that had already developed, as the earliest recorded mayor, Henry Fitz-Ailwin (d. 1212), is identified as such in a document of 1194 and is believed to have held office from 1189. The grant requires the mayor to be presented to the sovereign for approval and to take an oath to be faithful. These provisions have been respected ever since, and still govern the annual election and swearing in of the Lord Mayor. The charter carries a fine impression of John's Great Seal.

Just a few weeks after he granted this charter, John's enemies – noblemen who resented his taxation, unsuccessful wars and conflict with the Pope – forced him to agree to a new statement of principles on the rights of subjects and the limits of royal authority. This new Great Charter – Magna Carta – was a major step forward in defining individual freedom and the rule of law. Although its immediate intention was to end civil war, it has over the centuries achieved a worldwide symbolic status as one of the great documents of its kind. The first version of the charter was agreed to and sealed by John at Runnymede, in Surrey, in June 1215.

The charter was reissued and confirmed several times in the thirteenth century: the text that finally reached the statute book was not the 1215 version but a later one, granted by Henry III in 1225 and confirmed in Parliament in 1297. Of the twenty or so surviving thirteenth-century copies of Magna Carta, the City's, which dates from 1297, is one of the finest. The official statute wording is taken from the City of London's copy. One clause promises that 'the City of London may have all her ancient liberties and customs', and a clerk drew attention to the clause by writing 'n[ot]a' – 'note' - in the margin. London is the only town or city specifically mentioned in the charter, and the mayor was one of the twenty-five barons charged with securing its observance. The last few lines of text are obscured by the writ, originally separate but now sewn onto the charter, directed to the sheriffs of London commanding them 'to cause, without delay, the aforesaid charter to be published in the aforesaid city'.

As the seal is missing from all four surviving copies of the 1215 issue of Magna Carta, a mould taken from the seal of the mayoral charter was used in making the replica presented by the British Parliament to the US Congress to mark the bicentenary of American independence in 1976. **ES**

▲ **Letters patent of King John,**
granting the right to elect a mayor
Manuscript on vellum, with seal, 1215
LMA COL/CH/01/010

▲ Letters patent of Edward I,
confirming the liberties of England
(Magna Carta)

Manuscript on vellum, with seal, 1297
LMA COL/CH/01/021

The City's laws and charters

Liber Horn is one of the earliest illuminated manuscripts among the archives of the City Corporation, dating from the early fourteenth century. The book is a primary source for much of the documentary evidence for London history in the Middle Ages and for the development of medieval legal administration. Its 376 leaves contain a comprehensive collection of the statutes of Henry III (reigned 1216–72) and Edward I (reigned 1272–1307), together with numerous thirteenth-century legal treatises. It also includes a large and miscellaneous collection of London customs, ordinances of the City and the Guilds and a small collection of royal charters for London. The volume was clearly intended for practical use, and the text is corrected and annotated.

Liber Horn is made up of two separate parts, bound together perhaps around 1320, with the original binding still intact. An inscription within the volume records that it was made for Andrew Horn, fishmonger of Bridge Street, in 1311. The folio illustrated here offers further evidence of Horn's ownership: a shield of arms, depicting a fish and the saltire cross of St Andrew, is attached to a stem of foliage in the right-hand border.

Horn was born in London around 1275 and initially made his living as a fishmonger; he had a brother, Simon, in the same trade. He was warden of the Fishmongers' Guild in 1307, but that did not protect him from being sued in the same year for giving short weight in his fish baskets. He was no ordinary fishmonger, as he developed wider administrative and financial interests and was probably practising law by 1311. In 1320 he became chamberlain of the City, a post he held until his death in 1328. As chamberlain, it was his responsibility to defend the City's privileges, and during his term of office (and apparently earlier) he was responsible for compiling an impressive collection of documents, which he left to the City Corporation on his death. Regrettably, it is difficult to identify the other books he bequeathed among those surviving today. Some may have been dispersed, as other legal compilations of his can be found today in the British Library and in libraries in Oxford and Cambridge.

The role of chamberlain is one of the oldest and most important of the City offices. The earliest known holder was mentioned by name as chamberlain of London in 1237, but the function was certainly in existence by 1230 and possibly has its origin in the late twelfth century. The early chamberlains were drawn from the higher ranks of the citizenry, and several of them combined the post with that of an alderman. Many of the chamberlains were prominent members of the twelve great livery companies. The chamberlain, like all medieval financial officers, was held personally responsible for the City Corporation's money, which passed, or should have passed, through his hands. This personal responsibility was made clear by the appearance before the mayor and aldermen of the executors of the dead chamberlains, accounting for the revenues of the office and obtaining acquittances.

By a custom that operated from the thirteenth century to the eighteenth, the mayor and aldermen were responsible for granting custody of the City orphans (children of deceased freemen) to a guardian and to make sure their estate was secure. The chamberlain played a prominent part in this custom until the sixteenth century and from time to time even assumed personal responsibility for a child. For example, Andrew Horn became responsible for a vagrant City orphan in 1320 and looked after the child for eight years.

The chamberlain's duties included, in addition to collecting the City Corporation's revenues, the safeguarding of the records. Since the chamberlain was responsible for the City's cash, it is hardly surprising that valuable documents were entrusted to him. In the latter part of the fifteenth century this responsibility was transferred to the town clerk. **ES**

◀ ▶ Compilation of charters, statutes
and customs by Andrew Horn
Manuscript on vellum, 1311, fol. 204r,
and detail (left)
LMA COL/CS/01/002

Iste liber restat Andree Horn pysdenario
London de Bryggestrete in quo continentur
Carta et alie consuetudines istius Cunitatis.
Et certe libertates Angl. et statuta per hen-
ricum Regem et per Edlwardum Regem Alium
istius Regis Henrici edita.
Item fieri fecit Anno dm̄i. M. C C C x x.
Et Anno regni Regis Edlwardi filii
Regis Edlwardi. — xiij.

vicecomitati London

Edwardus dei gra̅ Rex Anglie dn̅s
hybn̄ Dux Aquitanie Archiepis Epis Abb̅s Priorib̅s Comit
baronib̅s Iusticiar vicecomit Prepositis Ministris et omnib̅s ballis
et fidelib̅s suis salt̅m. Inspeximus Cartam quam celebris memorie domini Henrici quondam Reg Angl pater noster fecit Civib̅s Londo-
nii in hec verba. Henricus dei gra̅ Rex Angl dn̅s hybn̄ Dux Norman et Aquitan Comes Andeg Archiepis Epis Abb̅s Comit baron
Iusticiar vic̅ Prepositis et omnib̅s ballis et fidelib̅s suis salt̅m. Sciatis
nos concessisse et presenti Carta n̅ra confirmasse Civib̅s London et co
itto cum omnib̅z rebus consuetudin que pertinet ad predm̅ vicecomit infra et
extra Civit̅ et extra p̅ aquas. Hnd et tenend eis et heredib̅z suis de nob et hered
Reddendo inde Annuatim nobis et hered n̅ris. CCC lj p̅ liberos bla̅
co̅s dn̅o̅b̅s dimme Ann. s. ad festum pasch. C. l. lj. Et ad festum
sci michis C. L. lj. Salvis Civib̅z London omnib̅z libtatib̅z et liberis con-
suetud suis. Et preterea concessim̅ Civib̅z London qd ipi de seipis
faciant vicecomites quoscumq̅ voluerint et amoveant Indecumq̅ voluerint.
Et eos qs fecerint vicecomites presentent Iustic n̅ris qui respondeant
nob ut Iustic n̅ris ad scc̅am de his que ad predm̅ vicecomit pertinent
et per quas nobis respondere debent. Et si sufficient respondeant et satisfecerint
Cives Londonienses respondeant et satisfaciant de crra et firma. Salvis eisdem
Civib̅z libtatib̅z suis sicut prius scriptum est. Et salvis eisdem vicecomit libtatib̅z que
alii Cives London h̅nt. ita s. qd bn̅ qui pro tempe fuerint vicecomites con-
stituti si aliq̅ debitum fecerint unde crra̅m firme debeant minorare non
dicentur ad plus ni ad crram̅ p̅ p̅ lj. et hoc sive catno aliorum Cium̅ et vic

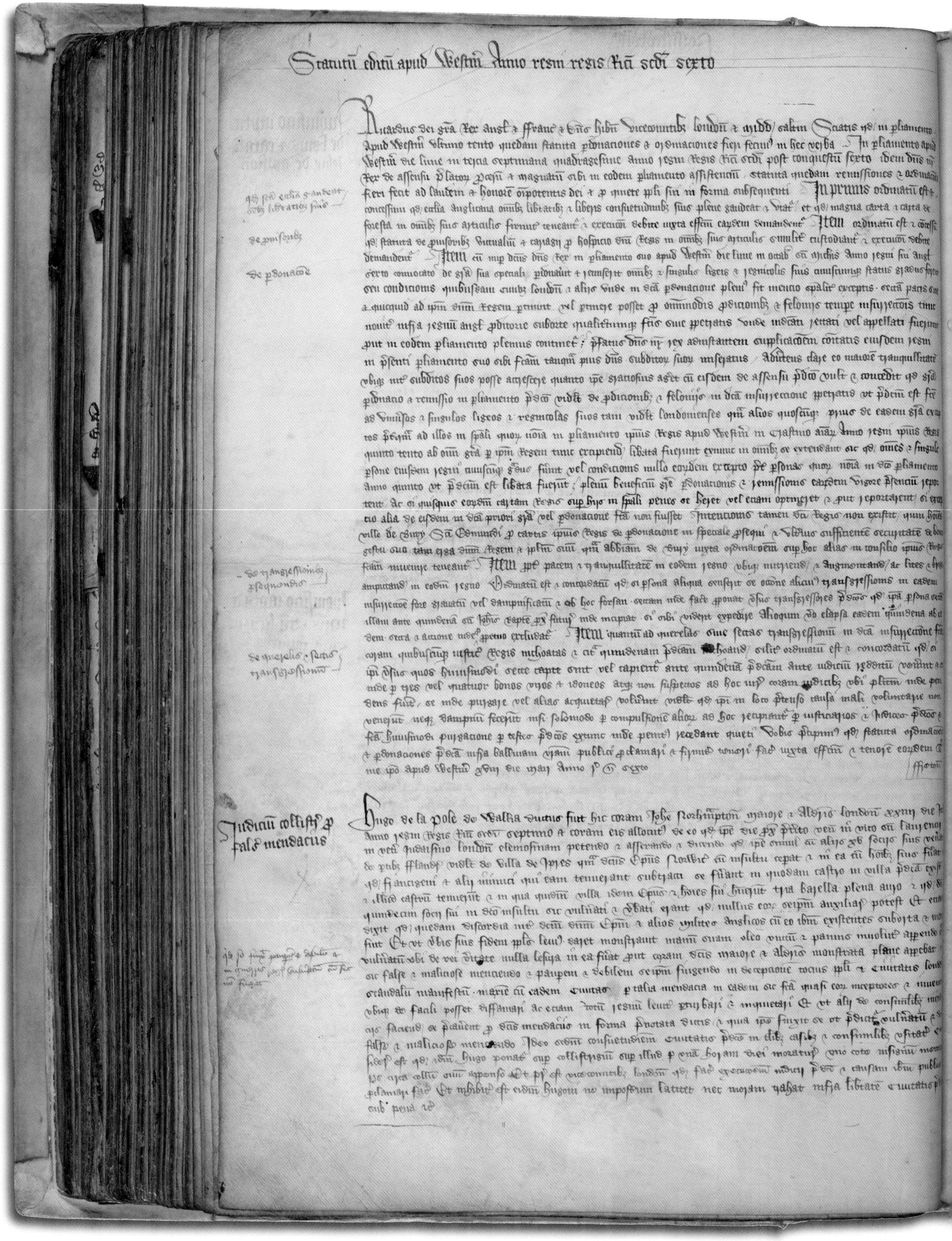

Ricardus dei gra Rex Angl & Franc & dns Hibn vicecomitibz London & aliis &c salutem. Sciatis qd in parliamento apud Westm ultimo tento quedam statuta pclamacones & ordinacones fieri fecim in hec verba. In parliamento apud Westm die lune in tercia septimana quadragesime Anno regni regis Ric oridn post conquestum sexto idem dns rex de assensu Prelatoy Procerum & magnatum ibidm in eodem parliamento assistencium statuta quedam remissiones & ordinaciones fieri fecit ad laudem & honorem oipotentis dei & p quiete ppli sui in forma subsequenti. In primis ordinatum est & concessum qd ecclia Anglicana omnibz libertatibz & liberis consuetudinibz suis plene gaudeat & vtat & qd magna carta & carta de foresta in omnibz suis articulis firmiter teneant & execucon debite iuxta essem eaydem demanden. Item ordinatum est & concessum qd statuta de huiusmodi victualiu & caristia p hospicio dni Regis in omnibz suis articulis omnino custodiant & execucon debite demanden. Item cum nup dns dns Rex in parliamento suo apud Westm die lune in octab sci Michis Anno regni sui Angl...

[body text continues, heavily abbreviated Latin]

...

Hugo de la Pole de Walha ductus fuit hic coram Joh Northampton maiore & Aldris London xxiiij die ... Anno regni Regis Ric ordni septimo & coram eis allocut de eo qd ipe die ... ...

Medieval administration

The series of volumes known as the 'letter books' document the earliest proceedings of the government of the City. They began in 1275, initially as registers of bonds and recognisances, but soon developed into administrative minute books, recording the meetings of the Court of Aldermen (illustrated here) and the Court of Common Council. They continued to be kept until the end of the seventeenth century and are called letter books because they were labelled with letters of the alphabet (not because they contained copies of letters). Fifty of these volumes survive, in continuous sequence, providing an essential quarry for the history of the City at both a micro and macro level. The pages shown here illustrate two events in the City's history.

The entry on the right, from 1285, represents an important step in the evolution of City administration as it provides the first list of forty 'probi homines' ('worthy and substantial men') who were to consult with the aldermen on the common affairs of the City. These reputable citizens were 'sworn of every ward', and the representation varied from one to three. This group evolved into the Court of Common Council, which became the main governing body of the City.

At this date the City had twenty-four wards (for the evolution of the wards see p. 22). Most of the wards are known by their modern names, allowing for some variations in spelling, the principal exception being the ward of 'Lodgate and Neugate' (Ludgate and Newgate), which is now known as Farringdon. The contemporary alderman of this ward was William de Farndone, and it is from his family surname that the modern name of Farringdon derives.

In 1322 it was agreed that rules to govern all citizens should be made by an assembly comprising two people from each ward, and in 1346 this was amended so that the number of representatives reflected the size of the ward. The court is first referred to as the Common Council in 1376, and by the end of the fourteenth century it had taken on a number of legislative functions, becoming particularly involved in financial affairs. As municipal services developed, so did the need to raise taxes, and the court became the representative body for the citizens in assenting to that. It has continued in existence ever since, gradually taking over more responsibilities from the Court of Aldermen. Its size has varied over time and by the nineteenth century had swollen to 240; today the Court of Common Council has a membership of 100.

On the left is a page from Letter Book H recording the writ to the City sheriffs pardoning those involved in the Peasants' Revolt of 1381. Triggered by years of discontent over the treatment of labourers, culminating in the imposition of a poll tax, this armed uprising was one of the most significant popular rebellions of medieval England, and its climax took place within the environs of the City. In June 1381 a large assembly of disaffected people, mostly from Essex and Kent, gathered at Blackheath, where they were inspired to action by the radical preaching of John Ball. The following day they stormed the Tower of London and summarily executed the Archbishop of Canterbury and the Lord Treasurer.

◀ City of London, Letter Book H
Manuscript on vellum, 1375–99, fol. 165v
LMA COL/AD/01/008

The young king, Richard II, agreed to meet the rebels at Smithfield. William Walworth, the Mayor, accompanied him and achieved fame by killing the rebel leader, Wat Tyler. The uprising collapsed, the ringleaders were captured and punished, and Walworth was knighted. To this day a dagger that is reputedly Walworth's is preserved in Fishmongers' Hall, and the Mansion House (the Lord Mayor's official residence) has a nineteenth-century stained-glass window depicting the scene at Smithfield. The rising itself went down in history as an early manifestation either of the fight for social justice or of the dangers of allowing radical ideas to foment (depending on perspective), and for centuries thereafter it was regularly re-enacted in City street theatre. ES

▲ City of London, Letter Book A
Manuscript on vellum, 1275–98, fol. 116r
LMA COL/AD/01/001

The wards and their aldermen

▲ Alderman of London
Watercolour on paper, *c.* 1447
LMA SC/GL/ALD

▶ St Paul's Cathedral, Cartulary, statute and evidence book (*Liber L*)
Manuscript on vellum, *c.* 1100–*c.* 1335, fol. 52r
LMA CLC/313/B/001/MS25504

The appearance of the ward as a unit of the civic governance of London is an ancient one, dating from at least the eleventh century. It was a military, judicial and administrative unit, the equivalent of the hundreds into which the countryside was divided, and ward boundaries are not usually the same as those of parishes. There were twenty-four wards in the City until 1394, when one more was added by dividing the largest, Farringdon, in two (the part within the City walls, and that without).

The first notices of wards usually record them by reference to their *ealdorman*, or alderman, an Anglo-Saxon term of hazy antiquity. The alderman was the pre-eminent citizen in the ward and represented it at City councils, later to become the Court of Aldermen. This has its origin in Anglo-Saxon folk moots, which also evolved into the Court of Hustings, for which there are references during the early eleventh-century reign of Canute. The aldermen have remained the most powerful figures in City governance, and the Lord Mayor is still picked from their ranks.

The oldest surviving list of these aldermen and wards in London is to be found in a cartulary of St Paul's Cathedral, known as *Liber L*, comprising a survey of the cathedral's London estates, made about 1127, and arranged by ward. In all, about twenty-three wards are recorded (some of the wording is unclear), most of them by reference to their alderman but some by local names: for example, 'warda alegate' (Aldgate) or 'warda fori' (Cheap Ward). It shows that the idea of geographical subdivisions certainly existed by this time but probably dated back well before the Norman Conquest.

A striking mid-fifteenth-century series of pen, ink and watercolour drawings shows us the complement of aldermen in the mayoralty of Sir Thomas Olney (1446–47). Each one stands holding a shield bearing his personal arms, while above a scroll records his name. The left hand rests on a large tablet bearing the arms of previous officers of the relevant ward, and the entire tablet is fitted with a nail, as though ready to be hung on a wall.

The outlines of the figures have been pounced, or pricked through, so that they can be copied from one sheet to the next; they are more heraldic records than attempts at accurate portraiture. The format of the drawings follows closely that of a similar series of representations of members of the Order of the Garter made around 1430 by William Bruges, the senior English herald. Facial characteristics are uniform, and the clothing changes little. The drawings are thought to be the work of Roger Leigh, Clarenceux King of Arms, and may have been produced in connection with a scheme for panelling, hangings or other decorations within the Guildhall precinct. Work on building the Guildhall had begun in 1411 and was well advanced by the time of Olney's mayoralty.

For many years these drawings were part of the Wriothesley heraldic collection, but by the twentieth century they were in the collection of Viscount Wakefield of Hythe, Lord Mayor in 1915–16 and a substantial benefactor to the library and art gallery. In 1938 he bequeathed them to the British Museum, but they were subsequently transferred to Guildhall Library.
MP, JS

parte orientali uirgultū . latitudinis . xxx . iiij . pedū .
longitudinis . lxxx iiij . pedū . & redditu in feud . ij . sol . in
festo sci onich . xij . d . opi . & xij . d canonicis . Socce Aldre-
manesberi . iij . ob . & j . d . regi in media quadragesima .

Terra Edrici clerici est longitudinis . quat̃ . xx .
pedum . ij . minus . in fronte latitudinis . xl . pedū . & redditu
in feud . xij . d . in festo sci Edmundi . Regi de soccagio . j .
d . Ex parte orientali t̃ra latior . ē . viij . pedibus .

Terra edmari reddit . ij . sol . in natiuitate sc̃e marie
Ex his reddunt regi . iij . d . in ramis palmar̃ . long q̃ter
xx xx . ped . latitudinis . lxxi . ped .

ꝛ Aldresmaneberi . Terra Wluredi reddit . iiij . sol in feud .
& . iij . ob socce . In fronte longitudinis . cxxx iiij . pedum .
latitudinis . xlj . peduꝝ .

ꝛ Warda fori terra Goduini scat reddit in feud . xx . sol .
longitudinis . c & xj . pedū . latitud . quater . xx . & . ij . ped .
De retro similiter quater . xx & ij . ped .

ꝛ Warda Edwardi parole terra sprot quā tenet Go-
dardus filius haroldi reddit . iiij . sol . Hec est in fronte latitudinis . lvij . ped . & usq: ad moram ptendr̃ lon
ante domū Taisonis tres mansure Egitudo .
reddunt . xviij . d . & una . iiij . d . in festo Scoꝝ Petri &
Pauli . quam terrā teneno Stephanus . Martinus .
Cilwinus . & Godid mater huiuet . longitudinis sec
uiam . c & xv . pedū . latitudinis . ci . pedis ex occidente . lx . pedū ex oriente .

ꝛ Warda Algari manningestepsune terra quā tenet
Adam reddit . iiij . sol & . viij . d . In pascha . & in festo
sci michaelis . In fronte secus uiam habet latitudinē
lv . pedū . longitudinē . c xl vj . pedum .

Terra Ascilli latitudinis secus uiam ab aqlonali parte
clj . pedis . longitudinis . c & quater . xx . & j . pedis ten-
dens ad meridiem . Et ex eadem terra secus uiā ex
occidente longitudinis . c & xxx iiij . pedū . latitudinis
lx iiij . peduꝝ .

ꝛ Warda Rad filii liuiue . Terra quā dedit Geroldus

The medieval legal framework

Cartae Antiquae is a late fifteenth-century volume of transcripts of charters and statutes of the realm, covering the laws enacted during the reigns of seven kings from Edward III in 1327 to Henry VII in 1485. It is written on fine vellum and richly illuminated. At the beginning of each sovereign's statutes is a royal portrait contained within the initial letter of the text, and a deep illuminated page border. We do not know who was responsible for its compilation, but the book would have been an essential reference tool for City officials.

The illumination is of a high standard but was evidently done in two stages, probably going to the same shop on each occasion. There is a distinct difference in portrait styles: one artist created the royal portraits for the statutes of Edward III up to Edward IV (d. 1483), while another did those of Richard III and Henry VII (reigned 1485–1509). The first artist, working probably in the 1460s, painted faces delicately, and his techniques and colouring are generally good, though his design is rather dated. His monarchs and their attendants do not show any perspective and are more of the playing-card

variety; his kings all wear an old-fashioned open crown, and all his figures have the short-cropped hair that was fashionable in the first half of the fifteenth century. The same colours were used by the artist of the last two portraits, who worked at some time between the mid-1480s and 1497. His colour-mixing figure work is less fine, with more crowded spacing, but he gave his kings the closed crowns and long hair expected at the time. The full leaf illustrated (right) contains the portrait initial for Edward III and is the work of the first artist; the detail (left) shows his image of Henry IV. The formal border around the text, of foliage twisted around a bar with an infill of pen-sprays, was standard ornamental work in England during this period.

The second artist was also certainly responsible for some crudely proportioned figures of kings and attendants with oversized hands in the historiated initials of a copy of the statutes 25 Henry VI to 11 Henry VII now at St John's College, Oxford. This manuscript has in turn been identified as bearing a remarkable similarity to another copy of the statutes held at Harvard University.

The inclusion of the City Corporation's coat of arms in the bottom border ensured that the volume was identified as a London book. The arms, a red cross on a white background with a sword in one of the upper quarters, are described in heraldic terminology as 'argent a cross gules, in the first quarter a sword in pale point upwards'. They have been used in this form since at least the late fourteenth century. There is a popular legend that the sword is meant to be William Walworth's dagger, used to stab Wat Tyler (see p. 21), but this is apocryphal; the sword is that of St Paul.

Parchment was the principal writing material of medieval Europe; writing with a quill on parchment required skill and practice. Other writing media included wax, used to make drafts or temporary notes. The choice of material was determined by the nature of the document being created and whether it was meant to be ephemeral or permanent; parchment was used for manuscripts intended to last. The purpose of the manuscript also determined both its shape and its size. Smaller books that were more portable would be used by officials in their daily business: larger ones were often used on a lectern to be displayed or read aloud. The large size of *Cartae* indicates that it was probably used for reference purposes, only occasionally, rather than on a day-to-day basis. **ES**

Henry IV

◀ ▶ Transcripts of charters and statutes, 1 Edward III to 11 Henry VII
Manuscript on vellum, 1327–1495,
fol. 37r, and detail of fol. 134v
LMA COL/CS/01/007

Ome hugh le despenser le piere ⁊ hugh le despenser le
fitz nasgains a la iointe Thomas adonges Count de lan-
caftre ⁊ de leicestr̃ Seneschal Dengletere ꝗ coie affent ⁊
agrée des piers ⁊ du poeple du Roialme ⁊ p̃ affent
du Roy Edward piere n̄re f̃ le Roy gorest come trartres
⁊ enemyes du Roy ⁊ du poeple fuiffent exilés deshen-
tés ⁊ baniz hors du Roialme ꝗ tantz iours puis ap̃s
mefmes ceux hugh ⁊ hugh p̃ malices counfeilt ꝗ le dit
Roy auoit pris de luy adonges ſauuz affent des piers
⁊ du poeple reuenerent en le dit Roialme ⁊ euro ⁊
aute aberzeient le dit Roi Edward a purſuiy le dit
Count de lancaftr̃ ⁊ aute grauntz ⁊ gentz du poeple
du Roialme volentiemen̄t ſuyent mort ⁊ deſhen-
tés ⁊ aſtuns vtlages baniz ⁊ deſherites ⁊ aſtuns deſ-
heritz ⁊ empriſonez ⁊ aſtuns gentz ⁊ deſhientz ⁊ apð...

en quelle p̃ſuite
le dit c̃oute de
lancaftr̃ ⁊ aut̃
gentz ⁊ gentz
du poeple du
Roialme

25

▲ Receipt from Richard Whittington and others for the purchase of the manor of Oxhey, Hertfordshire
Manuscript on parchment, with seals, 7 May 1402
LMA CLC/521/MS02903

The real Dick Whittington

Richard (or Dick) Whittington was one of the major figures of medieval London and a formative influence on the development of the City (and its library), quite apart from becoming the stuff of popular legend. The story of Whittington, the poor orphan who came to London to seek his fortune and who found it with the help of his cat and the sound of Bow bells recalling him, can be traced back at least as far as the early seventeenth century. It is wholly untrue, but Whittington himself was very real.

He was born in Gloucestershire around 1350, the son of a well-to-do landowner. He was apprenticed to a London mercer and thus entered one of the more upmarket trades of the time, dealing in wool, fine cloth and the flourishing import–export trade in such materials. He became a successful mercer himself and during the 1380s and '90s was regularly supplying extensive orders for luxury fabrics to the royal court. The fortune he thus accumulated allowed him to diversify into what we would now call banking, and he made many loans to the successive kings Richard II, Henry IV and Henry V.

He became a common councilman of the City in 1384, an alderman in 1393 and Lord Mayor in 1398. The one true part of the pantomime story is the reference to his being three times mayor, as he did serve again in this capacity in 1406 and 1419. During the last of these terms his attempts to regulate the price of ale and to standardise its measures brought him into dispute with the brewers. The City Corporation's archives include numerous documents relating to Whittington, such as the receipt shown here, with his seal appended. When he died, childless and a widower, in 1423, he left not only a reputation for probity but also a considerable fortune, all bequeathed to charity. Much of this was expended in benefits for the City, including the rebuilding of Newgate Prison (see p. 79) and of the south gate of St Bartholomew's Hospital, the installation of public fountains and the creation of the first Guildhall Library (see p. 27). **MP**

The first Guildhall Library

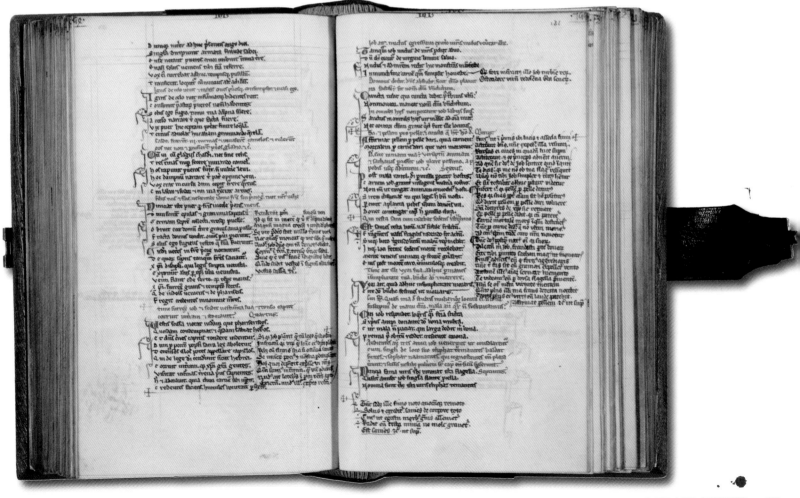

When Whittington died, in 1423, he left funds to be used for unspecified good works, at the discretion of his executor, John Carpenter, the clerk to the City Corporation. These bequests were supplemented by contributions from the executors of William Bury, another wealthy local mercer, who also died in 1423. One way in which Carpenter used these funds was in setting up a library attached to the Guildhall, which began operating around 1425. It has sometimes been called England's first public library, but it was probably envisaged as being primarily for the use of the priests of Guildhall College, a chantry college that originated in the late fourteenth century and was rebuilt in the fifteenth. We do know that wider access to the collection became available, as the chronicler Robert Fabyan (see p. 28) was allowed to borrow a manuscript of the *Chronicles of France*, which his widow's second husband had to return to the Corporation in 1516, three years after Fabyan's death.

This first incarnation of Guildhall Library survived little more than a century. The religious reforms during the reign of Henry VIII did away with the chantry college, and William Cecil, secretary to Lord Protector Somerset (with the reluctant if unavoidable consent of the Court of Aldermen), was sent to remove the whole collection in 1549, with empty assurances that it would be returned. It was not until 1824 that a public library was re-established by the Corporation.

We do not know how extensive the medieval library grew to be, but it was said to comprise three cartloads when taken away. There are only a few survivals, some in the City collections and others elsewhere. The library is likely to have had both printed and manuscript books, but none of the former is identifiable. This handsome manuscript of *Aurora*, a metrical version of the Bible originally written by the French poet and canon of Rheims Cathedral, Peter de Riga (d. 1209), was first given to the library by a certain master John Martil, according to a donation note that appears twice. This copy was probably written in England in the early thirteenth century. Its Guildhall provenance is confirmed by the reference in the inscription illustrated to the 'librarie co[mun]i Guyhalde Ciuitatis london[iarum]' ('the communal library of Guildhall, of the City of London'). The manuscript's whereabouts after its removal by Protector Somerset are unknown; it was bought back for the library in 1926. **MP**

▼ ▲ Peter de Riga, *Aurora*
Manuscript on vellum, early 13th century, pp. 148–49, and donation inscription on p. 340
LMA CLC/270/MS03042

Chronicling London

Robert Fabyan (*c.* 1450–1513) was the foremost chronicler of late medieval England. He is primarily known today for *The Newe Cronycles of England and Fraunce*, published first in 1516 and subsequently in 1533 as *Fabyans Cronycle Newly Prynted* (where his authorship was first established). The City Corporation owns two key primary sources relating to Fabyan's historical activity: an early sixteenth-century manuscript known as the *Great Chronicle of London* and a particularly interesting and extensively annotated copy of one of the most famous late fifteenth-century printed books, the *Liber Cronicarum*, or *Nuremberg Chronicle*.

Originally from Coggeshall in Essex, Robert Fabyan followed family members into trade in London, becoming a freeman of the Drapers' Company in 1476. He became a major civic figure: sheriff of London in 1493, alderman of Farringdon Without in December 1494 and twice Master of the Drapers' Company (1495–96 and 1501–02). In 1503 Fabyan resigned his aldermanship, on the pretence of lacking the means to take on the Lord Mayoralty, and retired to his country seat in Theydon Garnon in Essex, there to continue work on his two major chronicles.

The *Great Chronicle of London* is a handwritten account of London's history from 1189 to 1512. Fabyan continued the text from 1439, when the first, anonymous, author breaks off. The manuscript forms part of a corpus of London chronicles produced in the fifteenth century, each one borrowing from and influencing others, many of them possibly working from lost earlier chronicles. The *Great Chronicle* is, according to Charles Kingsford, writing in the early twentieth century, 'the fullest and most valuable of the London chronicles we possess'. It was for this reason he labelled it the *Great Chronicle*. It is sometimes cited particularly for its reference to the murder of the princes in the Tower on the orders of Richard III in 1483, which according to the *Chronicle* (and some other contemporary sources) was carried out by Richard's servant Sir James Tyrrell. This is the page illustrated here.

Fabyan's authorship of the second half of the *Chronicle* has been questioned, but the links between the manuscript and the printed *Nuremberg Chronicle* lay these doubts to rest. The latter is copiously annotated, including extensive lists of London office holders and marginalia relating to London affairs. It does not contain Fabyan's name, but it does include his personal coat of arms and that of his livery company, the Drapers, drawn in at the beginning. The marginalia are written in the same hand as the latter part of the text of the *Great Chronicle* (as well as in the two surviving manuscript portions of the *Newe Chronicles* as printed in 1516), proving Fabyan's role in each of the works.

The *Nuremberg Chronicle* (as it is generally known in England) is one of the most celebrated fifteenth-century printed books, not least for its 1,809 woodcut illustrations. These are the work of Michael Wolgemuth (at one time Albrecht Dürer's master) and Wilhelm Pleydenwurf. The text describes the history of the world, from the biblical Creation to the time of the author, and contains much contemporary detail about European countries and cities. As published, the woodcuts were all in black and white – printing illustrations in colour was a nineteenth-century development – but in Fabyan's copy they have all been hand-coloured to a high standard. We do not know whether Fabyan executed this himself, but the colouring is of his time.

There are numerous copies of the *Nuremberg Chronicle* in libraries around the world (including others in Guildhall Library), but this copy is exceptional for the extent and quality of the individual additions made after it left the printing house, including Fabyan's extensive annotations and the note on the flyleaf, in his hand, that he bought the book on 3 April 1495, for what was then the very considerable sum of sixty-six shillings and eightpence (£3 6s. 8d). This is the earliest precisely dateable purchase inscription known for any copy of this book. **MP**

▼ Robert Fabyan, *The Great Chronicle of London*
Manuscript on paper, *c.* 1490–1512, fol. 213r
LMA CLC/270/MS03313

◀ ▶▶ Hartmann Schedel,
Liber Cronicarum
Printed in Nuremberg, 1493
Copy with early hand-colouring,
owned and annotated by
Robert Fabyan from 1495, fol. 1v
and (overleaf) fols 47v–48r
LMA CLC/270/MS03789

Alomon ascendit in Gabaon vt immolaret in excelso vbi erat tabernaculum et altare eneu Moyf
obtulit mille hostias in holocaustum. Et apparuit ei dominus in nocte per somnium dicens vt p
teret quod vellet ab eo. Is postulauit sapientiam ad regendum populum suum. Placuit sermo
ram domino et ait. Cuz non petieras diuitias gloziam et moztem inimicozum seu longam vitam exaudit
es. Dedi tibi coz sapiés cp nullus ante similis tui fuerit ¶Primumcp iudicium in quo ostensa est sapientia
fuit de duabus meretricibus habentibus filios. Quozum vno a matre nocte oppzesso contendebat de s
stite cuius esset. Et data sententia per Salomonem cp diuideretur in duas partes: rogauit mater vera cp
tus viuus daretur potius alteri mulieri. Et ex hoc iudicauit Salomó esse illá verá matré sibicp dari iussu

Iudicium Salomonis

Emplum domini toto ozbe celeberrimum Salomon rex anno quarto regni sui edificare cepit. cp si
it. cccc lxxx. egressionis israel de egipto. A natiuitate abzahe nongentesimus octuagesimusquart
Et in octauo anno compleuit. Fuit autem edificatum in hierusalem in monte mozia vbi abzahas v
luit filium immolare. et Jacob vidit in somnis scalam de celo ad terram. Id autem templum ex lapide alb
totum constructum fuit. Cuius fabrica multa arte confecta est videlicet de lapidibus politis mira arte co
positis. Eius longitudo cubitozum sexaginta fuit. Latitudo viginti. Et altitudo centum viginti. Et cuz h
dispositione cp a pauimeto iuxta terram vscp ad pzimum tabulatum erat altitudo. xxx. cubitoz. Et a pzim
tabulato seu solario vscp ad scóm erat altitudo. xxx. cubitozum. Et ab isto scdo solario vscp ad tercium quo
erat tectum templi erat altitudo sexaginta cubitozum. Habebat ergo duo solaria inter pauimentum et tec
Et in quolibet solario et in tecto erat ab extra in circuitu deambulatozium. Istud dicitur in euangelio pi
culum: super quod xps a dyabolo tentatus fuit. Et erat ibi cancelli ante ne inde caderent ambulantes. Et
uidebatur in duas partes scz in sancta ad quê locum pzimo erat ingressus in templum ex parte ozientis. p
cubitozum. Et sanctasanctozum. xx. Eratcp in medio inter sancta et sanctasanctozû paries factus tabulis
drinis. Et postea lamis aureis cooptus altus. xx. cubitis. Ante quem velum appensum tenue pulcherri
intextum. quod scissum est a summo vscp deozsum tempoze passionis. Intra sancta sanctozum erat archa
mini facta a moyse. In archa erant tabule decalogi. Solum semel intrabat summus sacerdos in anno in sa
ctasanctozum infesto pzopitiationis cum magna solennitate. In sancta autem circa velum intrabant sepe
li sacerdotes in certs sacrificijs ad accendédas lucernas. Et tibi ex pte meridionali erat candelabzáz aureü
fecerat Moyses cum septem lucernjs. Et ex pte Aquilonari mesa pzopositionis. In medio aut erat altare au
um factú a Moyse. sed addidit Salomó. x. alia candelabza eiusde scematis sed maiozis quátitatis. quicp a
dextrá. z quicp ad sinistrá. Et similiter. x. mesas aureas maiozes. Et in medio altare thimiamitis.

Templum Salomonis

Menpriaus.

Anni mũdi — 4062°

Linea pontificũ

Sadoch filius achitob

Sadoch summus sacerdos in principio regni Salomonis sedere cepit. Hic fuit in nũero pontificum octauus.

Achimaas filius sadoch

Achimaas nonus sumus hebreorū sacerdos clarus fuit. et maxime veneratiõe apud iudeos habitus est.

Achias ppheta

Achias silonites ppha pdixit hieroboã q esset rex sup. x. tribus isrl.
Iste Hieroboã dece scissuras pallij ab Achia ppha accipies z in egiptũ fugies. mortuo Salomõe a dece tribubus elect in regez Uitulos aureos cõflatiles in dan z neptali posuit ydolatra pessimus effectus. peccare fecit isrl pplm ad ydolatriã iducedo. Uñ totius ppli isrl destructio secuta é.

Semeias

Semeias ppha compescuit Roboã ne pugnaret cõtra Hieroboã. z scripsit eoz regũ gesta. Iste etiaz pphauit qñ Sesac rex egipti diuersa mala fecit terra iuda anno scz quinto roboam.

Nadab hieroboã regis filius scõs israheliaz rex incepit regnare scõ anno Aza regis Iude et fecit malũ sic pater eius. Et pcussit euz baassa z regnauit p eo scõm pphetiã Achie pphe.

Addo ppha hic pphauit cõtra uitulos aureos z manus hieroboã arui í via a leone iterfectus é.

Iste Baasa de tribu Isachar terci israhelitaz rex fecit malũ corã dño ambuládo in oĩbus pctis hieroboã nec audiuit Hieu ppphetaz ad eũ missuz ß occidit eũ z ipe a chreõe pept.

Ela baase regis filius qrtus regũ isrl Illũ interfecit eius seruus Zambri

Addo propheta

cũ omni domo pris sui usez mingentem ad parietem scõm prophete dictum.

Linea regũ israel

Hieroboam

Nadab

Baasa

Hela

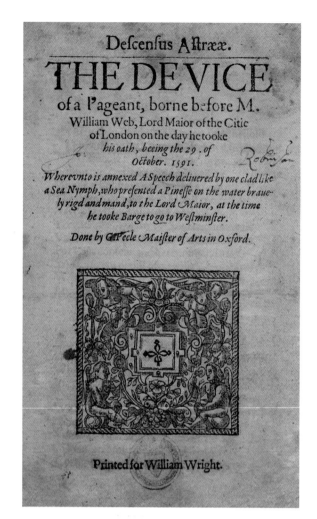

Descensus Astraeae.

THE DEVICE

of a Pageant, borne before M.
William Web, Lord Maior of the Citie
of London on the day he tooke
his oath, beeing the 29. of
October. 1591.

Wherevnto is annexed A Speech deliuered by one clad like
a Sea Nymph, who presented a Pinesse on the water braue-
ly rigd and mand, to the Lord Maior, at the time
he tooke Barge to go to Westminster.

Done by G. Peele Maister of Arts in Oxford.

Printed for William Wright.

◀ George Peele,
Descensus Astraeae
Printed in London, 1591,
title page
GHL SR

▼ Worshipful Company
of Grocers, Account book,
charges of triumphs
Manuscript on paper, 1613–41,
detail of fol. 14v
LMA CLC/L/GH/D/036/MS11590

City pageantry

Processions and theatrical displays have long been an important part of civic life. Marking significant events such as coronations, inaugurations and anniversaries with festivals and civic ceremonies helps to bond the people with the governing agenda; Roman emperors understood the importance of circuses for all. The City has always known how to use such activities to encourage civic harmony, and there is a long history of celebrating key events with ceremonial entertainment. The Lord Mayor's Show (see p. 39) continues this tradition to this day; shown here are some records of pageantry from the turn of the seventeenth century.

Stephen Harrison's *The Arch's of Triumph* was published in 1604 to celebrate the lavish procession through London, from the Tower to Temple Bar, made by the newly crowned James I earlier that year. The volume includes exquisite plates by the Dutch artist William Kip, portraying the seven temporary triumphal arches that were erected in a memorable conceit intended to surpass even the increasingly elaborate artistry of the annual Lord Mayor's pageant. Odes, to be read at each arch, were composed by writers including Thomas Dekker and John Webster.

The pageant held in 1591 to mark the inauguration of Lord Mayor William Webb is uniquely recorded in the Guildhall Library copy of *Descensus Astraeae* (the only known example of this printed pamphlet to have survived). Its author, George Peele (1556–1596), might almost be said to have been born into a City pageant, since his father, James, had earlier had special responsibility for their production. One of Peele's first works was the mayoral pageant for 1585, *The Device of the Pageant* (the earliest printed pageant pamphlet to survive), and he may have been responsible for others in the 1580s. *The Device* prints only the speeches, which was the custom until *Descensus Astraeae*, in which for the first time an explanation and description of the spectacle were given.

The image of Astraea, the Just Virgin of the Golden Age, whose return was foretold in Virgil's Fourth Eclogue, pervades Renaissance political thought, but it was identified particularly with Elizabeth I by her subjects. In Peele's work she is represented as a reforming shepherdess.

The growing industry surrounding such pageants and displays is reflected in the accounts for events contained among the archives of the livery companies of each new Lord Mayor, which were required to organise and pay for them. This included payments for painters and carpenters, musicians and actors, as well as provision for food and drink and costumes. Important playwrights were regularly commissioned to write the speeches and devise the spectacles. Ben Jonson, Anthony Munday and, perhaps most successfully, Thomas Middleton regularly organised proceedings. In 1617, for example (as shown here), Thomas Middleton was paid £282 for 'ordering, overseeing and writyng' *The Pageant of Nations* for Sir George Bolles. **MP, JW**

▶ Stephen Harrison, *The Arch's
of Triumph*
Printed in London, 1604, p. [4]
GHL A.5.2/20

LONDINIVM

Maximus hic Rex est
v luce serenior ipsa
Princeps qua talem
Cernit in Urbe ducem
Cuius Fortuna superat
si Unica Virtus. Ve

DOMVS HAEC COELO SED MINOR EST DOMINO

1 2 3 4 5   10

A monarch in trouble

The archive collections of St Paul's Cathedral, deposited with the City Corporation, provide a rich window on to all aspects of the cathedral's life over the centuries. Like all major archives, its contents are not wholly predictable, and this remarkable document is a fragment of national history as much as church history and an insight into the personal struggle of Charles I towards the end of his reign.

In April 1646, towards the end of the English Civil War, Charles was in a desperate plight, besieged in Oxford after suffering a series of heavy defeats to Cromwell's New Model Army. Trying to rescue the situation, he offered to strike a deal with the Almighty that 'if it shall please his divine majesty of his infinite goodness to restore me to my just kingly rights, and to re-establish me in my throne, I will wholly give back to his Church all those impropriations which are now held by the Crown'. On 27 April, Charles disguised himself as a servant, escaped from Oxford and handed himself over to the Scottish army in the hope of forming an alliance. That hope soon proved futile; the following year he was returned to the custody of the English Parliament, and in January 1649 he was executed.

This pledge was drafted for and signed by Charles, but a more formal version was never produced during the frenetic final days at Oxford. Instead this record of the vow was kept secretly by Gilbert Sheldon, Charles's chaplain, who buried it and kept it hidden for thirteen years. It was not until 1660, when the monarchy was restored with Charles II, that Sheldon revealed it. Two months later he became Bishop of London, and in 1677 Archbishop of Canterbury.

The document eventually made its way into the hands of Edmund Gibson (1669–1748), who also became Bishop of London and Archbishop of Canterbury. Gibson's papers were put up for sale in the nineteenth century, and the librarian of St Paul's, W. Sparrow Simpson, purchased the collection for the cathedral library. **JG**

▲ Charles I's vow to restore
Church property
Manuscript on paper, 1646
LMA CLC/270/MS25762

A Restoration Lord Mayor

This portrait of Sir John Robinson, Lord Mayor in 1662, shows a successful City man in Restoration London, when the return of Charles II after the turbulent years of the Civil War and Interregnum promised better stability and security. Robinson (1615–1680) was born in Leicestershire and after apprenticeship to a London clothworker became a freeman of the Clothworkers' Company in 1645. Thus began a distinguished City career, bringing great wealth. He was Master of the Clothworkers' Company in 1656 and a City sheriff in 1657.

Robinson represented the City in the 1660 Parliament and in the same year was created a baronet and appointed Lieutenant of the Tower of London. The restored king, who was godfather to one of Robinson's children, wanted trusted allies in the City's government and is believed to have personally requested that Robinson accept election as Lord Mayor in 1662. His support for Charles was not only political, as he used his wealth to make much-needed loans to the Crown finances.

This portrait reflects Robinson's simultaneously held offices as Lord Mayor and Lieutenant of the Tower. The mayoral 'SS' collar (see p. 12) is lying on a table covered with a richly coloured Turkey carpet, while the White Tower is seen through the window. Depicted in full periwig, crimson sash, embroidered coat and military breastplate, he carries both a sword and a knobbed stick. Samuel Pepys, who knew Robinson well, found him a 'vain, prating, boasting man', and there is plenty of self-assurance in this portrait; but as his *Oxford Dictionary of National Biography* entry points out, 'his bombast must have concealed political shrewdness and commercial acumen'. **JJ**

▶ John Michael Wright, *Sir John Robinson, Lord Mayor 1662*
Oil on canvas, c. 1662
GAG 1836

The City and the Irish Plantation

The City has long had strong links with Northern Ireland. At the beginning of the seventeenth century James I sought to build on the Tudor conquest of Ireland through 'plantation', involving the deliberate supplanting of the local (mainly Roman Catholic) population with imported Protestant workers and families. The City Corporation was exhorted to play a leading role, and although reluctant to be drawn into something so politically and economically dubious, refusal was not an option. The response was to make the best of it by trying to turn the situation into a business opportunity.

The Society of the Governor and Assistants, London, of the New Plantation in Ulster, within the Realm of Ireland was formed in 1609 and incorporated in 1613. It managed the City's involvement, specifically to oversee the plantation of the area around the small town of Derry in north-west Ulster. The 1613 charter turned Derry into a city and defined a county around it, both renamed Londonderry. The livery companies were drawn in to help finance and run the outlying estates, and the new county was divided into twelve 'proportions', each managed by one of the 'great twelve' companies, aided by a group of minor companies. The society retained specific jurisdiction over the cities of Londonderry and Coleraine.

Each partner in the venture took an active role in the management of their estates and produced voluminous documentation, including maps. The first surveys date from 1613, and they were variously copied and updated; the map here is an eighteenth-century assessment of the Ironmongers' Company lands. The hazards of the local territory (the countryside was dangerous, and the locals even more so) meant that much of the surveying was little more than imaginative guesswork; the mapmakers did not set foot in large areas of the country.

Political and economic manoeuvring saw the dissolution of the society and the termination of the City's involvement in Northern Ireland in 1639, when Charles I claimed the lands as forfeit. The society was reconstituted by Charles II in 1662 and rechristened The Honourable The Irish Society. Unfortunately, the Great Fire of 1666 destroyed the royal charter, and the society had to obtain the replacement shown here in 1667.

Despite a changing role, The Honourable The Irish Society has been actively involved in the area ever since and maintains links between the cities of London and Derry. Extensive and important records relating to the early (and more recent) history of Ulster can therefore be found among the collections, both in the archive of the society itself and in those of the livery companies. The Irish Chamber, built in 1824 as the society's administrative headquarters, is one of the few remaining pieces of nineteenth-century architecture in Guildhall Yard. **MP**

▼ Charter of Charles II reconstituting The Honourable The Irish Society
Manuscript on parchment, 1667, first membrane
LMA CLA/049/AD/13/007

▶ Plan Book of the Irish estates (Lizard manor) of the Worshipful Company of Ironmongers (detail)
Manuscript on parchment, c. 1725
LMA CLC/L/IB/G/097/MS17298

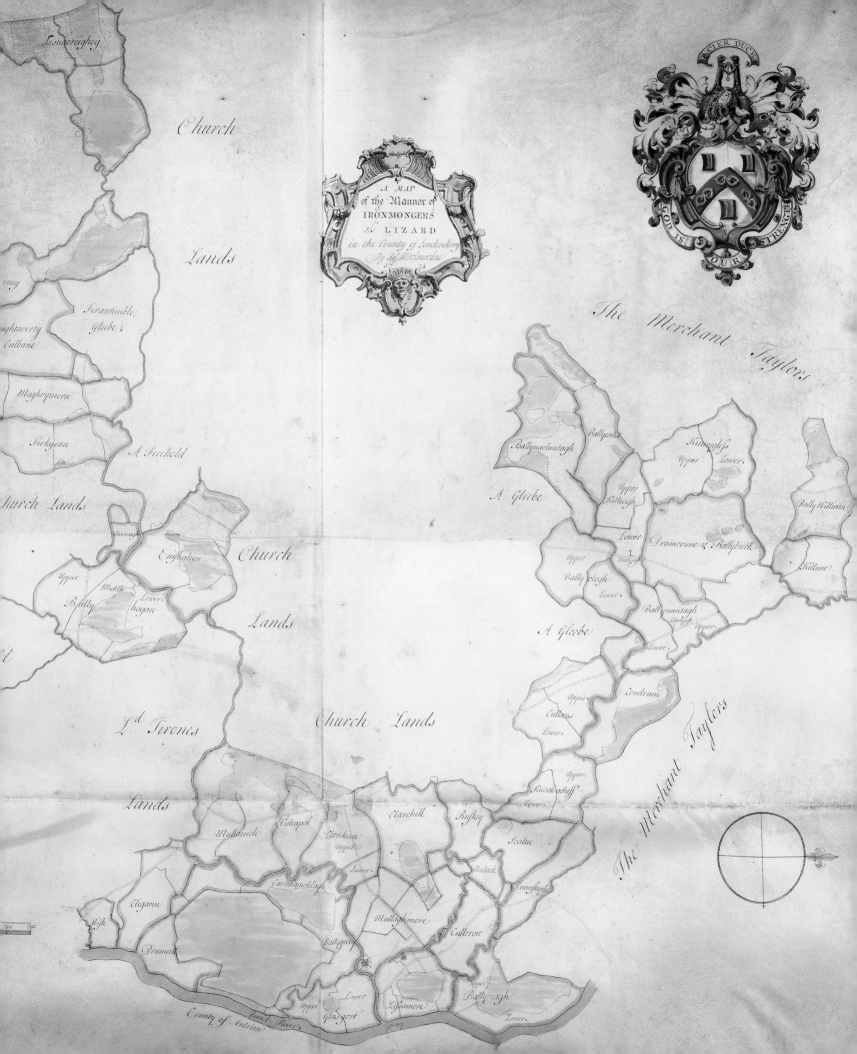

Lisnacreaghog

Church

Lands

Church Lands

Serantimble
Glebe

Culbane

Maghrymorn

Sirkyran

A Freehold

Church Lands

Upper
Middle
Lower
Ballyhagan

Inishatien

Kincreagh

Ld Tirones

Church

Lands

Church Lands

Lands

Mullanen

Cilcapil

Clonkeen
Upper

Lower

Clarehill

Rasky

Carnanucklagh

Cligann

Rysk

Drumedl

Ballyguy

Mullaghmore

Calleron

Upper
Glasgort

Lower

Lissamore

Lower

Ballyragh

County of Antrim

Band River

A MAP
of the Mannor of
IRONMONGERS
als LIZARD
in the County of Londonderry
By Jn Macdanachan

The Merchant Taylors

Ballynacluntagh

Ballycaht

A Gleebe

Upper
Killeagh

Lower
Earlspit

Upper
Bally clegh
Lower

A Gleebe

Kinnaglefs
Upper   Lower

Drumerune & Ballybreck

Ballynuntagh
Ballyspill
Upper
Lower

Ballywilliam

Killure

Upper
Cullans
Lower

Condrum

Upper
Knockaduff
Lower

The Merchant Taylors

Scattie

Clenback

Drumslappe

ACIER DUCE

GOD IS OUR STRENGTH

America and liberty

The City has various historic links with America; City men were involved with the Virginia Company, which colonised Virginia, and established Jamestown, in the early seventeenth century. By the second half of the eighteenth century, relations between Great Britain and her American colonies were deteriorating. Britain's claim to tax her colonies was symbolised by the tax on tea, and in 1773 the tea ships lying in Boston Harbour were attacked and their cargo flung into the sea (the 'Boston Tea Party'). In September 1774 all the American colonies agreed to combine in stopping trade with Britain until their grievances were redressed, and in 1775 open war broke out.

The City Corporation was strongly opposed to the policy of the British government. In January 1775 the Common Council of the City gave warning, in petitions to both Houses of Parliament, of the consequences of the government's actions and the antagonism they would arouse in America. The views of the City were well known in America, and on 5 May 1775 the Committee of the Association of New York wrote to the Lord Mayor and Corporation with an appeal to the City to use its most vigorous exertions to 'restore union, mutual confidence and peace to the whole Empire'.

The forty signatories to this letter included Isaac Low, the chairman of the committee, and John Jay, lawyer, diplomat and first Chief Justice of the United States. Similar views were expressed in another letter from the American Congress at Philadelphia (illustrated here), appealing to the City as the 'patron of liberty', signed in the bold hand of John Hancock, president of the congress and later first signatory of the Declaration of Independence. The strength of pro-British feeling was such that the Corporation could make little headway, but it continued unrelenting in its disapproval when open hostilities broke out. When peace came at last, in 1783, and the independence of the United States was formally acknowledged, the Court of Common Council prepared an address congratulating George III on having paid 'final attention' to the petitions of his faithful citizens and people, expressing the City's firm conviction that the commercial interests of Britain and North America were inseparably united.

Among the City voices arguing for American liberty, one particularly notorious one was that of John Wilkes (1725–1797), who spent the decade of the 1760s in and out of prison for his outspoken attacks on George III and British government policy. Expelled from Parliament in 1769, he found friends in the City, where he was elected an alderman in the same year. In 1774 he was elected Lord Mayor, and his incumbency was a factor in prompting the American letters. Guildhall Library has a special collection of Wilkes material, including not only printed works by or about him but also a small number of books from Wilkes's own library, with his bookplate. **ES**

◄ Letter from the American Congress to the Lord Mayor and livery companies of London
Manuscript on paper, 29 September 1775
LMA COL/SP/07/012

► Bookplate of John Wilkes
Engraving on paper, c. 1770
GHL Wilkes 075

The Lord Mayor's Show

The Lord Mayor's Show has a long history, rooted in the requirement for each year's newly elected Lord Mayor to present himself to the sovereign, at Westminster, to swear allegiance. His journey developed into an occasion for a grand procession, with pageantry and public entertainment, and today's Lord Mayors still lead an annual carnival parade through London, every November, in a gilded state coach.

Two rather different representations of the show, a century and a half apart, are reproduced here. Hogarth's famous urban fable on *Industry and Idleness* concludes with the industrious apprentice Francis Goodchild elected Lord Mayor. Hogarth's take on his triumphant ride along Cheapside is not altogether reverent; the City marshal, with sword raised but hat falling over his eyes, together with the preened footmen clustering for position behind the coach, suggest that civic *gravitas* may not run all that deep. Hogarth always liked to remind his viewers that pride comes before a fall.

William Logsdail's painting of the Lord Mayor's procession in 1888 (overleaf) is a more serious affair. As the footmen

stride in front of the Royal Exchange, a varied (but more respectful) crowd looks on. Logsdail, who painted several large-scale London views during the 1880s, was keen to make the spectators as authentic as possible. An orange seller, a soldier, a minstrel and various children have prime positions, while slightly further back someone tries to crush the top hat of a tall gentleman who is blocking the view of the less well-placed spectators.

The Lord Mayor for 1888–89, Sir James Whitehead, was noted for his humanitarian views, and for his wish to use City funds to support the poor and deprived of London. His mayoralty was something of a watershed year for the City, as it saw the creation of London County Council and the beginning of a decade of much debate over the possible amalgamation of the Corporation with London government more widely. The London Government Act of 1899 brought this to an end, and the preservation of the City Corporation as an administrative unit ensured that the Lord Mayor's Show also continued to be an annual feature of London life. **JS, NA**

▲ William Hogarth,
The Industrious 'Prentice Lord-Mayor of London
Engraving on paper, 1747
LMA SC/GL/SAT/003

▶▶ William Logsdail,
The Ninth of November, 1888
Oil on canvas, 1890
GAG 1091

◄ Banquet menu for the reception, at Guildhall, of the Shah of Persia
Lithographic polychrome print on silk, with paper lining, 1873
LMA COL/RMD/CE/01/019

ENTERTAINMENT
TO HIS MAJESTY
THE SHAH OF PERSIA
AT THE
GUILDHALL,
Friday 20th June 1873.

BY THE
RIGHT HON. THE LORD MAYOR
AND THE
CORPORATION OF THE
CITY OF LONDON.

MENU

PURÉE DE VOLAILLE.   POTAGE À LA VICTORIA,

SAUMON À LA ROYALE.

FILETS DE TRUITE À LA SEFTON.   CHARTREUSE À LA MODERNE.
RIS DE VEAU SAUTÉ AUX CHAMPIGNONS.
SUPRÊME DE VOLAILLE À L'ÉCARLATE.
CÔTELETTES D'AGNEAU AUX PETITS POIS.
CROUSTADES DE CAILLES À LA REINE.
POULET FARCIS AUX RAISINS DU SOLEIL.

ASPIC DE FOIES GRAS DE STRASBOURG.   SALADE À LA RUSSE.

PEACOCKS DISPLAYED.

GALANTINE DE VOLAILLE AUX TRUFFES DE PÉRIGORD.
PÂTÉ À LA GODARD.   LANGUE DE BŒUF.
QUARTIER D'AGNEAU RÔTI.
ALOYAU DE BŒUF À LA PRINCESSE ROYALE.
POULETS RÔTIS À L'ESTRAGON.

SUÉDOISE DE FRAISES À LA CRÈME.
PÊCHES À LA BELLE-VUE.
GELÉE AU VIN DE MADÈRE.   CRÈME AU MARASQUIN.
GATEAU À LA PRINCESSE.   COMPOTE D'ANANAS.
PATISSERIE À LA BOHÉMIENNE.
BOMBE GLACÉE.

The ALBION,   Aldersgate Street.

THE RIGHT HONOURABLE SIR SYDNEY H. WATERLOW, KNT. LORD MAYOR
Sheriffs: { THOMAS WHITE ESQ ALDERMAN. Under Sheriffs { ARTHUR TURNER HEWITT ESQ
           FREDERICK PERKINS ESQ   ALEXANDER CROSLEY ESQ
M. Mc GEORGE ESQ CHAIRMAN

State ceremonial

The City Corporation has for centuries entertained royalty and visiting heads of state. When the Holy Roman Emperor Charles V visited England in 1522, he was greeted by the Lord Mayor and aldermen, and it was common for the City authorities to be notified of the arrival of foreign ambassadors so that they could provide suitable lodgings and assistance during their time in London.

During the nineteenth century state occasions became more frequent, and the Corporation was called upon regularly to host state receptions on behalf of the government, a role that remains important today. Many such events are well documented in the archives, and the reception of His Imperial Majesty Nasser al-Din Shah Qajar, the Shah of Persia, held in Guildhall on 20 June 1873, is a particularly lavish example.

On 24 April 1873 the Court of Common Council appointed a reception committee to plan a memorable celebration with 'an amount of splendour' as would befit the 'ruler of so ancient an Empire as Persia'. The accounts show that £15,429 was spent on the evening (equivalent to c. £705,000 today), with three thousand guests invited, including members of the royal families of both nations, great officers of state, ambassadors and ministers, peers, Members of Parliament, judges, consuls, mayors, masters of livery companies and a host of other civic worthies.

At a little before ten o'clock in the evening, the Shah, escorted by a detachment of the Royal Horse Guards, arrived at Guildhall in the Queen's carriages. The event began with the presentation of an address to the royal guest, followed by a grand ball, with music provided by the bands of the Grenadier Guards, the Coldstream Guards and the Royal Artillery. The entertainment ended with 'supper' (a rather casual description of a meal comprising nine courses and twenty-six individual dishes), which for the royal party was held in the Council Chamber.

As an indication of the political importance of such official entertainments, Queen Victoria bestowed a baronetcy on the Lord Mayor (Sir Sydney Waterlow) for hosting the event, and the two sheriffs received knighthoods. Nasser al-Din Shah himself was appointed a Knight of the Order of the Garter, the highest English order of chivalry. **HD**

▼ Admission ticket for the reception, at Guildhall, of the Shah of Persia
Chromolithograph and manuscript on paper, 1873
LMA COL/RMD/CE/01/019

◀ Certificate of the City's resolution of thanks to Arthur Wellesley, Duke of Wellington
Manuscript on vellum, 7 July 1815
LMA COL/CHD/FR/08/01/083

Honouring statesmen

The City Corporation's archives include numerous handsomely decorated documents recording the bestowing of honours. From 1792 onwards, anyone granted an honorary freedom of the City was given an illuminated certificate, of which duplicates were made and kept in the Chamberlain's Court. The Duke of Wellington is an example of someone whose services to the nation, in defeating Napoleon, were rewarded several times by the City.

On 9 May 1811 Wellington was awarded the honorary freedom of the City of London with a sword of the value of 200 guineas. The following year, in recognition of his victory at Salamanca, Common Council passed a resolution of thanks to Wellington and added a gold box to the freedom of the City already accorded to him. Following victories over the French near Vitoria, another resolution was passed by Common Council on 12 July 1813.

Following the Treaty of Paris in May 1814, Wellington was entertained at the Guildhall on 9 July 1814, and the opportunity was taken of presenting him with the freedom, which he had hitherto been unable to take up, as also with the sword of honour and gold box. Following the great victory at Waterloo, Common Council passed another resolution of thanks in 1815, and it is this illuminated resolution that is illustrated here. ES

Wining and dining

Although dining has always had an important role to play in civic as well as private life, it is important to avoid excess. This lively satirical print, by an artist known to us only as 'M.G.', gives visual form to a concern that may from time to time have troubled office holders in the City. Assailed by the insistent attentions of the fish, fowl and flesh that he would be expected to consume during his year (and with only two bottles of champagne with which to defend himself), the Lord Mayor of 1830, John Key, suffers in anticipation of the task before him. A lobster bites his nose.

Satires lampooning the perceived indulgence of members of the London civic community occur on a regular basis from the mid-eighteenth century. Hogarth included some noticeably voracious diners in a print from his 'Industry and Idleness' series of 1747 (from which another image is shown on p. 39), when 'the industrious prentice [is] grown rich & sheriff of London'. Rotund aldermen and guzzling liverymen always made an easy target for the cartoonist's pen.

The publisher of this particular print could not have foreseen the events that would unfold in the days immediately preceding the Lord Mayor's Banquet of 1830. In line with tradition, as the first major City banquet in a new reign (that of George IV), the King, Queen and royal family were among the invitees along with the Prime Minister (the Duke of Wellington). However, John Key, the incoming Lord Mayor, nervous that public disorder might follow the presence of the Duke (whose strong resistance to reform was extremely unpopular in the City), wrote to the King expressing his concerns, and cancellation soon became inevitable. The City was dismayed, and Key was vilified for his shaky reaction to the situation.

The Lord Mayor's Banquet has medieval origins. The early festivities were held at the halls of livery companies and were lively occasions, at which jesters might perform various antics, such as leaping into bowls of custard. Guildhall became the setting from 1501, and the events progressively became more dignified and serious. Today the banquet is held shortly after the Lord Mayor's Show and is attended by the Prime Minister of the day, who makes a speech on foreign policy.

The City Corporation archives include an impressive run of civic banquet menus and invitation cards from the late eighteenth century onwards. Along with beautifully printed and embossed invitations are menus detailing the quantity of food provided. Thus we know that (as a body) nineteenth-century banqueters would routinely consume more than two hundred tureens of turtle soup, several barons of beef, hundreds of jellies and a vast weight of pineapples. **JS**

▼ 'M. G.', *Fatal Effects of Gluttony:*
A Lord Mayor's Day Night-Mare
Lithograph, 1830
LMA SC/GL/PR/SAT/1830

A coronation luncheon

The banquet held in Guildhall to celebrate the coronation of Elizabeth II on 12 June 1953 was an altogether happier occasion than John Key's aborted banquet of 1830 (see p. 45). This canvas, by Sir Terence Cuneo, who was also commissioned to paint the official coronation scene in Westminster Abbey, was presented to the City by Sir Sidney Fox, who was one of the sheriffs in that year. The Lord Mayor for the year, Sir Rupert de la Bere, can be seen in the middle of the top table, between the Queen and the Queen Mother.

The painting follows in the long tradition of celebrating the pomp and pageantry of royal progresses, coronations, jubilee celebrations and other state and City functions, but the coronation took place at a time of post-war austerity. In advance of the banquet the *City Press* speculated hopefully on the prospects of better times ahead:

> The most eagerly awaited feature of the City's Coronation celebrations is the day of the Queen's progress to the Guildhall to be entertained to luncheon by the Lord Mayor, Sheriffs and the Corporation. For over 700 people the most eagerly awaited feature of that day is the luncheon itself. Not only will they be able to tell their families, children and friends how they once attended this occasion, but also a Guildhall banquet conjures up for them dreams of a profusion of good food. Dare we hope that food rationing will be so relaxed by the time of the Coronation that a baron of beef will be available for all those at the Guildhall luncheon? It was the practice of those attending great dinners in the past to carry away what could not be eaten on the spot for the family. The end of meat rationing might properly be celebrated in conjunction with the Coronation of Queen Elizabeth II by the reappearance of barons of beef and of this ancient habit.

On the extreme left of the painting a chef can be seen carving just such a baron of beef, so the City Corporation did not disappoint in honouring the tradition.

Terence Cuneo was a highly successful twentieth-century painter, born in London in 1907 to parents who were themselves graphic artists. His skills and preference for a style that was more representational than conceptual brought him many commissions, and he developed a reputation for painting engineering subjects, particularly railways. He was also well known for landscapes, horses and military action (he was a War Artist, as well as a sapper, during the Second World War). From the late 1950s onwards (so not here) he developed a sometimes mischievous trademark by including a small mouse somewhere within his paintings. He died in 1996, and the Terence Cuneo Memorial Trust was set up shortly afterwards to create a permanent memorial to his life and work. JJ

▶ Terence Cuneo, *The Coronation Luncheon to Her Majesty Queen Elizabeth II in Guildhall, 12 June 1953*
Oil on canvas, 1953
GAG 1507

CHAPTER TWO

The Engine of Finance

Commerce and the City have long been closely inter-twined. Today the Square Mile is one of the leading international hubs of the financial services industry, and the City Corporation plays an important role in facilitating and advocating the growth of such an important part of the British economy. The emergent City in the early Middle Ages came into being because the site of Roman Londinium was a natural location for a trading settlement, well placed for transport by land and water. It evolved into a centre that was both a national focus of business activity and a model for local regulation of interdependent trades. The gradual establishment of wide-reaching services that became economic cornerstones, such as the Royal Exchange, the Bank of England, Lloyd's and the Stock Exchange, confirmed the place of the City at the heart of national commercial enterprise.

The nineteenth century was a time of great transformation in the City's business character, when the medieval inheritance of multiple small enterprises built around individual trades was gradually replaced with financial institutions. Shopkeepers and merchants moved out, while bankers, insurance traders and financiers moved in. This changed the social fabric of the City as a place; the bankers, unlike the shopkeepers, were commuters rather than residents, and the population of the Square Mile declined from about 130,000 at the beginning of the nineteenth century to less than 30,000 by the turn of the twentieth (now it is about 9,000). These developments laid the foundations of the City as we know it today.

The collections naturally reflect these key aspects of City life. Seventy-eight of the 108 livery companies have deposited their archives with the City Corporation, to make them available for study and to ensure their safe stewardship. This relationship is just one aspect of the long history of close connections between the Corporation and the companies, whose liverymen still take part in the election of the City sheriffs and Lord Mayor. The terminology derives from the custom, which developed during the fourteenth century, whereby senior members adopted distinctive robes (liveries) to be worn on special occasions. Entry to one of the companies was normally through apprenticeship. After serving a period of training, usually seven years, apprentices became freemen of their company.

Until the nineteenth century freedom in this sense was an essential prerequisite for anyone wishing to exercise a trade, or keep a shop, in the City. Freemen enjoyed a range of rights and privileges, including the ability to vote in ward elections and immunity from tolls.

These livery company collections, dating back to the twelfth century, not only contain a great wealth of material on the development and management of trades but also include treasures such as the illuminated Fraternity Book shown opposite. About a quarter of the ancient companies have records earlier than 1400, and three-quarters of the seventy-eight deposits include material before 1600. While documenting the development of the companies as such, these archives also encompass social and biographical details of many City inhabitants and take in numerous charitable foundations, schools and hospitals supported by the companies.

Beyond the livery companies, the collections include a huge range of business archives and material related to commercial activity; there are over 5 kilometres of shelving devoted to the records of City-based firms at London Metropolitan Archives, from the fifteenth century to the present day. The Stock Exchange archives, held on deposit, include a great wealth of material on applications by companies to trade in shares, as well as information about individual brokers. The maritime industry is extensively chronicled in the records of Lloyd's of London, with information on the movement and loss of shipping over several centuries. The archive collections are complemented by important holdings of printed material, such as the trade directories and runs of insurance- and exchange-related periodicals, which are a particular strength of Guildhall Library.

The items reproduced in this chapter have been chosen from across these various sources, supplemented by graphic material depicting the development of some of the major financial institutions. They show how business records can be valuable not only for economic historians but also for all kinds of social historians; the Sun Fire Office albums, with their photographic record of parts of the world that have long since been transformed, are an excellent example. The wealth of advertising and ephemeral material to be found in business records, which can be useful for designers today, is also illustrated here.

Medieval guild wealth

Many of the great medieval livery companies had special volumes to record their rules and ordinances, sometimes including the text of the oaths sworn by all new members. Expensively made and richly decorated, these books reflected the honour, prestige and wealth of their guilds. This handsome miniature, depicting Elizabeth Woodville, wife of Edward IV, comes from the Book of the Fraternity of the Assumption of Our Lady of the Skinners' Company.

The Skinners received their first charter in 1327 as a result of the more general use of furs and the consequent growth of abuses in connection with the trade. Ordinances for the regulation of the trade were drawn up immediately prior to the granting of the first charter and again in 1365 and 1676. The company continued to control the English fur trade until the eighteenth century. Skinners' Hall, at 8 Dowgate Hill,

existed before 1295. It was burnt down in the Great Fire, rebuilt in 1670 and refaced in 1790.

The Book of the Fraternity of the Assumption of Our Lady, which contains the ordinances and annual lists of wardens and members of the Fraternity, was initially copied by a single scribe around 1441, and was thereafter enlarged and continued by a series of scribes. The lists are lavishly illustrated and are important as they show a succession of dateable border styles of illuminators working in London from 1487. The decoration shown here is the finest of a number of miniatures and full-page pictures. Others include a smaller portrait of Margaret of Anjou, wife of Henry VI, and a full-page illumination of the Virgin Mary crowned among the saints in Heaven. **PS**

▲ Elizabeth I, Charter to the
Worshipful Company of Blacksmiths
Manuscript on vellum, , 20 April 1571
LMA CLC/L/BD/A/001/MS02962

The livery companies

The symbiosis between the livery companies and the City Corporation is a historic and important one, and the archives of the companies, many of which are deposited with the Corporation, constitute a hugely valuable seam of primary source material for the economic and social history of London. The companies evolved both as mutual support bodies, for individuals undertaking a particular occupation, and as trading standards organisations; maintaining professional standards helped to regulate competition. Although their role has changed since the nineteenth century, with more emphasis on charitable and educational activity, the livery companies continue to play an important part in City life.

As the guild system developed between the twelfth and fourteenth centuries, companies increasingly sought to obtain a degree of protection before the civic authorities by means of royal charters. As well as being the legal means by which companies could act as a corporate body, such charters were also signs of wealth and power. They benefited both the company, by offering legitimisation, and the Crown, by providing a source of income. The need for such stamps of royal authority meant that the accession of a new monarch usually prompted the expeditious acquisition of a new charter (with the appropriate fee paid to the royal coffers).

The charter of Henry II to the Weavers' Company is by some way the earliest surviving manuscript belonging to a modern livery company. It can be dated by reference to the witnesses – Thomas Becket, as Chancellor, and Warin FitzGerald – to some point between 1155 and 1158. In it the King grants the weavers their guild in the City of London, with all the liberties and customs they possessed in the time of Henry I, and prohibits anyone from practising the craft, either in or around the City, unless they are a member of the guild, on pain of a fine of £10. This shows that some kind of guild structure was in place as early as the mid-twelfth century, and probably earlier. To lobby for and obtain a royal charter the formative Weavers' guild must have had members with officials to represent them, and funds, as well as somewhere to meet and store their goods.

The charters themselves became increasingly long, ornate and expensive, the work of a number of limners, scribes, painters and clerks. By the sixteenth century the borders were often a riot of decoration, intertwined foliage and motifs, sometimes incorporating the companies' coats of arms (themselves symbols of status and rank). The opening initial usually displayed the royal patronage at work with a handsome portrait of the monarch. As such they were very much documents drawn up for prestige, to be displayed in the company halls, as some still are. This reaffirmation of the rights and liberties of the Blacksmiths' Company, issued when Elizabeth I came to the throne in 1558, is a nice and characteristic example. MP

▲ Henry II, Charter to the
Weavers' Company
Manuscript on vellum, c. 1155
LMA CLC/L/WC/A/001/MS04621

Trade and exchange

Commerce has always depended on opportunities to meet and trade, and has been facilitated by the establishment of recognised centres where those looking to buy and sell can congregate. The earliest public building erected specifically for financial and commodity trading was the Antwerp Bourse, built in 1531, and its success prompted Sir Thomas Gresham, a leading sixteenth-century merchant, to create a similar facility for London. He agreed to build it, at his own expense, provided that the City Corporation purchased a suitable plot; the aldermen agreed, and in 1571 Queen Elizabeth I formally opened what was thereafter known as the Royal Exchange.

The Exchange has seen three architectural manifestations. The original building was destroyed in the Great Fire of 1666, and its replacement in another fire in 1838 (see p. 114). Wenceslas Hollar's print shows the first Exchange during a typical day, with several hundred City brokers and traders gathered. Some of the costumes reflect the overseas dealing that was a major part of life in the Exchange; then, as now, international networks were a vital element in building prosperity. The gathering is almost exclusively male; the only woman to be seen is a seller of broadsides.

Trading in stocks and shares of companies such as the Bank of England (see p. 54), or in speculative overseas trading ventures, evolved during the seventeenth century and grew thereafter. The dealers in stocks began congregating separately, originally in coffee houses in Exchange Alley on the other side of Cornhill from the Royal Exchange, and eventually in the Stock Exchange, founded in 1773. The trade in securities, from the end of the seventeenth century onwards, is chronicled in *The Course of the Exchange*, first published by John Carstaing in January 1698 and issued twice-weekly thereafter. Prices for exchange in a number of European cities were shown, as well as figures for commodities and various stocks.

Throughout the eighteenth century publication of the list was continued by several business partners and relatives of the Carstaing family. The drive to raise capital for the expansion of railways in the nineteenth century brought a new price list, the *London Daily Railway Share List*, to join the *Course of the Exchange* and a third list, the *Foreign Stock List*, which covered overseas companies and stocks. In January 1867 the Stock Exchange Share and Loan Department began issuing the *Daily Official List*, which by the late nineteenth century had expanded to cover a vast range of companies, government stocks and bonds. Consolidation of the titles occurred over time, and today only the *Daily Official List* survives, published electronically. Guildhall Library possesses a virtually unbroken series of these various lists from 1698 to the present day.

The River Thames underpins London's pre-eminence as a port for the import and export of goods worldwide. In the early eighteenth century the river wharves and docks were bustling with activity fronting a busy thoroughfare for local, national and international traffic. Illustrated below is a sample from the extensive collection of early business records at London Metropolitan Archives. It shows a page from William Brooke's bills of lading that relates to cargo sent from London to Barbados. The ships, masters and consignees are recorded, along with detailed information on what was sent in each shipment. The volume of bills covers the period from 1696 to 1709, and records Brooke's consignments mainly to Barbados, but with occasional shipments to Bermuda and Rotterdam. Brooke is most probably William Brooke (1662–1737) of St John Square, Clerkenwell, who became a director of the South Sea Company in 1721 and who amassed a fortune estimated at his death to be £80,000. **AH, JS, RW**

▼▼ *The Course of the Exchange* (detail)
Printed in London, 1701
GHL Store

▼ Bill of lading relating to William Brooke's trade between London and Barbados
Print and manuscript on paper, 1701
LMA CLC/B/227/MS18472

▶ Wenceslas Hollar, *Interior View of the Royal Exchange* (detail)
Engraving on paper, 1644
LMA SC/GL/PR/512/ROY(1)ext

Honoratissimo Domino,
PRÆTORI REGIO sive MA=
iori, Iohanni Wollaston, Eqviti,
Amplissimoq & Prudentissimo Sena=
tui, Nobilissimæ & Florentissimæ Rei
publicæ Londinensis. Itemq
Duumviris, seu Vice-Comitibus
eiusdem Civitatis; IOANNI FOWKE
IACOBO BVNCE: hanc suam ta=
bellam humillimè. D.D.D.
Richardus Daynes.
1644

BYRSA LONDINENSIS,
vulgo
The Royall Exchange of London.

En LONDINENSIS, totum celebrata per orbem,	Lo heere the Modell of Magnificence,
BYRSA, decus Regni nec minor Vrbis Honos.	Th EXCHANGE of LONDON thorough EVROPE fam'd,
Nobile GRESHAMI fuit hoc opus, ELISABETHA	Erected first by GRESHAMS greate expence,
REGALE hanc voluit dicier esse suum.	And by the Roial'st Queene the ROYAL nam'd
Omnigenæ hic prostant merces, hic Gallus Iberus	The mother Antwerps farre exelling, where
Ruthenus, Cimber Teutog, conveniunt.	But emptines is seene, or trifles sold.
Quas his quoq die lata excipit area murus	Arabian odors, Silkes from SERES heere,
ANGLORVM REGVM splendet Imaginibus	Pearles Sables, fine linnen, Iewels, clothes of gold
Sed nihil hæc est tot pulchris habitata puellis	And what not rare or rich our kinges take place,
ut Venerem huc credas, transposuisse PAPHON	Without, Within a World of beautieous faces,

H. Pecham.

it is to be vnderstand for the fourth Walke, beeing such as thother three, arched, & such Pillors as the rest. All which could not bee heere conveniently exprest. W: Hollar fecit Londini. Anno 1644.

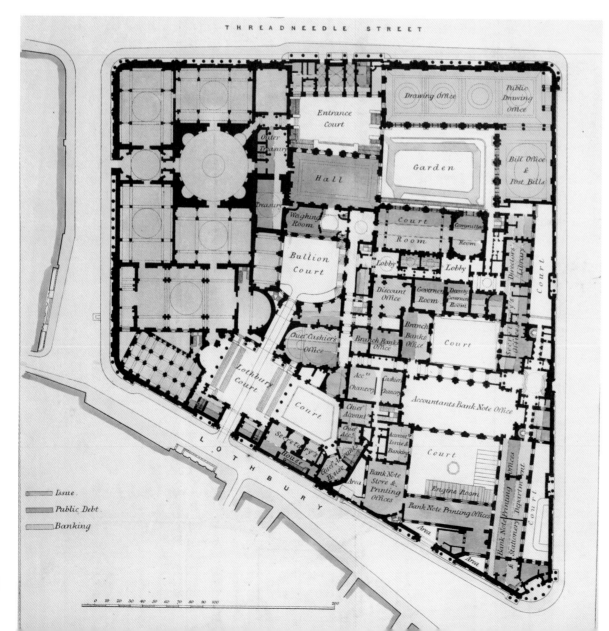

THREADNEEDLE STREET

▲ Augustus Pugin and Thomas
Rowlandson, *The Great Hall of
the Bank of England* (detail)
Aquatint on paper, 1809
LMA SC/GL/PR/044/BAN

◀ *Plan of the Bank of England*
Lithograph on paper, published
by Malby & Sons, *c.* 1840
LMA SC/GL/PR/044/BAN

The Bank of England

The Bank of England occupies a prominent place not only in the business history of the City (and indeed the nation) but also architecturally: its familiar monumental edifice dominates the junction of Threadneedle Street, Cornhill and Poultry, facing the Royal Exchange and the Mansion House. It has a long history and evolved gradually into the national central bank we know today, and a model for such banking systems around the world. The Bank was a private company until 1946, when the Bank of England Act brought it into public ownership.

The Bank was founded in 1694, initially as a mechanism to raise money for the Crown to support war. The Nine Years' War, which began in 1688 and drew England into an alliance of European states against France, saw the French defeat a joint English and Dutch fleet in the Battle of Beachy Head in 1690. It was recognised that the English navy was weak and desperately in need of investment, for which there were no public funds. In 1694 Charles Montagu, 1st Earl of Halifax, set in motion a plan to establish 'the Governor and Company of the Bank of England', whereby shareholders would generate £1.2 million as a loan to the government. In return, they received interest, set initially at 8 per cent per annum.

The Bank's role developed throughout the following century; the loan was not paid off but grew as more and more loans to the government were made, thus creating the concept of the National Debt. By the time the Bank's charter was renewed in 1781, it was known as the public exchequer. As well as loaning money to the government, it became a mechanism for supporting other banks by holding deposits and providing funds, thus evolving into the hub of the national banking system.

The right to issue banknotes was an integral part of the original scheme, but the Bank did not originally have a monopoly on this. In 1844 the Bank Charter Act gave the Bank of England sole national rights for the issue of banknotes, although some private banks retained existing privileges until the 1930s. The earliest notes were handwritten, but they began to be printed in the second quarter of the eighteenth century.

The Bank's first premises were in Mercers' Hall, and then Grocers' Hall, but in 1732 the Bank moved to Threadneedle Street to take over the mansion of Sir John Houblon, its first Governor. A new, classically designed building was created for it by the architect George Sampson and then much enlarged by Sir John Soane at the end of the eighteenth century. During the second quarter of the twentieth century it was rebuilt again, to designs by Sir Herbert Baker; although Baker paid homage to Soane's neoclassical ideas, the view of architectural historians has generally been that much elegance was lost. Nikolaus Pevsner, in his *Buildings of England* volume for the City of London, described it as the worst individual loss of London architecture during the twentieth century.

The Bank retains its own archive, and its primary documentary history therefore remains in Threadneedle Street. The City Corporation's collections do, however, include a range of material relating to the Bank and its interaction with other organisations, as well as graphic sources that chart its development. Benjamin Cole's mid-eighteenth-century engraving shows a bird's-eye view of the building before Soane, while Pugin and Rowlandson's illustration gives us a snapshot of the interior fifty years later. The mid-nineteenth-century ground plan shows the complexity and scale of the interior, including courtyards and a garden.

The aquatint of the Great Hall is one of a series of illustrations produced for *The Microcosm of London*, one of the great early nineteenth-century colour plate books issued by Rudolph Ackermann, a German publisher who settled in London and established a reputation in this field. Intended to showcase the city as a whole, the book was published in parts between 1808 and 1810, with illustrations combining the work of Thomas Rowlandson, who drew the figures, and Augustus Pugin, who used his skill as an architectural draughtsman to provide the buildings and backgrounds. **ST, DP**

A Perspective View of the Bank of England.

▲ Benjamin Cole, *Perspective View of the Bank of England*
Engraving on paper, c. 1750
LMA SC/GL/PR/044/BAN

Lloyd's and insurance

When Edward Lloyd first established a coffee house in Tower Street in the 1680s, he could scarcely have dreamt that one day the name 'Lloyd's' would signify one of the world's leading centres of insurance broking. By 1692 he had moved premises, to the corner of Lombard Street and Abchurch Lane, and gradually his coffee house acquired a reputation as the place where those connected with the maritime trade – merchants, shipowners and ship's masters – came to obtain shipping information.

Lloyd died in 1713, leaving the coffee house to his son-in-law, and it continued to be a hub of information exchange around shipping. In 1769 a group of professional underwriters set up the New Lloyd's Coffee House in Pope's Head Alley, laying the foundation of Lloyd's as the recognised marketplace for insurance business. A few years later, in 1774, they moved into the Royal Exchange (see p. 52).

The reputation of Lloyd's coffee house was greatly enhanced by the publication of *Lloyd's List* as a reliable source of shipping information. It is thought to have first appeared in 1734 – the report of a Lloyd's subcommittee in 1837 stated that it had existed for 103 years – but the earliest surviving issue is that of 2 January 1740/41, numbered 560, illustrated here. Originally weekly, by 1741 it was being published twice a week. The publication days, Tuesdays and Fridays, are thought to have been chosen because it was on those nights that the foreign mails were dispatched. Guildhall Library holds a run of the *List*, with some gaps, from 1741 to date.

This first known issue of *Lloyd's List* consists of a single sheet with miscellaneous commercial information on the front page and the shipping news, headed 'The Marine List', on the verso. Only English and Irish ports are listed, and, with the exception of three departures from Cork, only arrivals are noted. The details given are the port and date of arrival, the name of the vessel and that of its master.

The first item of shipping news appeared in the next issue, on 6 January: the *Roehampton* from Nevis and the *Lloyd* from St Kitts 'both drove out in the storm the 30th Aug. are arrived safe at Jamaica, and both loading there for London'. Shipping arrivals were also reported from foreign ports such as Leghorn (Livorno), Antigua and Montserrat. Gradually the number of ports covered and the number of shipping casualty reports increased, so that by 1792 *Lloyd's List* could be described as being 'universally received all over the country as the Gazette of Ship News'. It is still being published today, on a daily basis, as an essential source of current information for anyone connected with maritime business.

Lloyd's of London remains today a hub of the international insurance market; its 'inside-out building' headquarters in Lime Street, designed by Richard Rogers and opened in 1986, is one of the iconic features of the modern City streetscape. The firm deposited its historic marine records, both manuscript and printed, on permanent loan at Guildhall Library in 1979. Since that date further deposits have been made, including administrative, medal and signal station records. This collection thus constitutes an outstanding resource for maritime history from the eighteenth century to the present day. **VH**

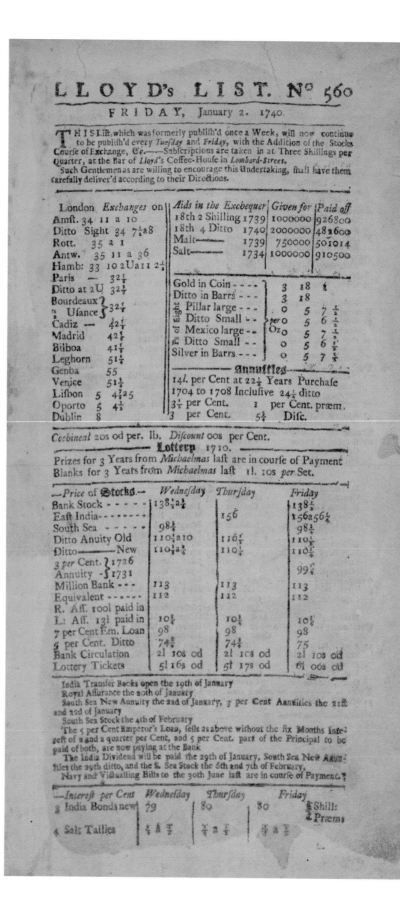

▲ *Lloyd's List*, no. 560 (Friday 2 January 1740)
Printed in London, 1741 (before 1752, the new year began on 25 March, not 1 January)
GHL SR 5.4

Loss of the *Mary Celeste*

Lloyd's loss and casualty books, deposited in Guildhall Library by Lloyd's of London (see p. 56), contain brief reports of shipping casualties, entered on a daily basis as they were received. Invaluable for marine and family historians, their brief entries hide no end of human tragedy at sea, from the loss of well-known ships such as the *Titanic* to the endless lists of now forgotten vessels. The page illustrated here contains one of the more celebrated listings, for the *Mary Celeste*, better known as the *Marie Celeste*, a name that has become a byword for the inexplicably deserted.

No hint of her extraordinary story or subsequent fame is contained in this matter-of-fact entry, but the known facts of her fateful voyage are soon told. Under the command of Benjamin S. Briggs this American brigantine left New York on 7 November 1872, bound for Genoa with 1,701 barrels of alcohol. On 5 December the British brigantine *Dei Gratia* sighted a vessel that proved to be the *Mary Celeste* 'under short canvas, steering very wild and evidently in distress'. Three crew members were sent to investigate and render assistance if necessary.

On board they found not a living soul. The lifeboat was missing, together with navigation instruments and ship's papers, but personal effects such as oilskins and tobacco pipes remained. All the signs pointed to a hasty but orderly evacuation of the vessel some time on or after 25 November, when the last entry on her log slate recorded her off Santa Maria, in the Azores. What puzzled the *Dei Gratia*'s men, and later aroused the suspicions of the authorities, was that there was no obvious reason for her abandonment. The ship was well provisioned and seaworthy, and there was no obvious evidence of mutiny or piracy.

The loss book notes that three men of the *Dei Gratia* brought the empty ship into Gibraltar. The findings of a subsequent Vice-Admiralty court were inconclusive. The likeliest reasons for a vessel to be abandoned were problems with the cargo or the ship taking on too much water, but if either of these had been the explanation in this case, the perceived danger had not materialised. Released by the court, the *Mary Celeste*, under Captain Blatchford, was cleared from Gibraltar on 7 March 1873 and finally reached Genoa on 21 March. No trace of her crew was ever found, and no wholly satisfactory explanation as to why ten people abandoned an apparently seaworthy vessel in mid-ocean has ever been advanced.

The loss and casualty books are only one part of the extensive archive of material from Lloyd's that make it possible to trace the movement and sinking of ships since the eighteenth century. Some of these relate specifically to wartime losses. The archive also includes useful biographical material relating to the maritime world, such as the Captains' Registers, which list captains or mates of boats who held British masters' certificates between the mid-nineteenth and mid-twentieth centuries. These list not only the men and the dates of their certificates but also the names and official numbers of the vessels on which they served. **VH**

▲ Lloyd's loss and casualty book
no. 19: entry for 14 December 1872
Manuscript on paper, 1872, fol. 699
GHL CLC/B/148/B/004/MS14932/031

A
COLLECTION
OF THE
MERCHANTS
Living in and about
the CITY of LONDON.

[A.]

Robert Abbot, *Bow-Church-*
yard.
Allen Ackworth, *Burchin-Lane.*
Edward Addams, *Great St. Bar-*
tholomews.
John Addis, *Bednal-Green,* or at
the *Sun* in *Lumbard-Street.*
Elias Adrian *and Company* in *Broad-*
street.
Thomas Allcock, *in Grubstreet.*
Richard Aley, *Mincin-Lane.*
B   Richard

◀ *A Collection of the Names of*
the Merchants Living in ... London
Printed in London, 1677, fol. B1a
GHL SR

▼ Trade card for Robert Stone,
nightman
Engraving on paper, 1755
LMA SC/GL/TCC/RYL-TOR

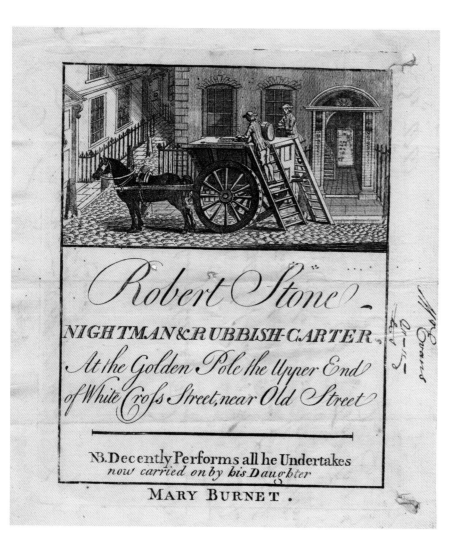

Advertising trade

From the seventeenth century to the twentieth the published directory was an indispensable source of information on merchants and trades. It also included selective lists of private residents from the mid-nineteenth century. Guildhall Library has one of the largest collections of historic British directories not just for London but also nationally, with local editions for counties and provincial towns and cities. As survivals they are rare, since they were intended to be ephemeral, discarded when a new edition appeared. Directories not only help to identify individual names but also show changes to localities over time.

Although it was not the first published list of London inhabitants, *A Collection of the Names of the Merchants Living in and about the City of London* (1677) is the first publication that can properly be described as a directory. Compiled by Samuel Lee, it comprised an alphabetical list of some 1,900 merchants, with the streets on which they lived or worked.

Over fifty years passed before James Brown compiled the next London directory, published by Henry Kent in 1734. Thereafter directories were issued for London on a regular basis by various publishers. Resentment arose when the Post Office brought out its *New Annual Directory*: its semi-official status gave it an unfair advantage. Frederic Kelly acquired the copyright of the *Post Office Directory* in 1837, and *Kelly's Directories* came to dominate the genre. Their lively advertisements, alongside lists of businesses, trades, streets and residents, make them an invaluable quarry of social history.

Advertisements have always been important for selling wares, and trade cards are among the earliest manifestations. They provided a cheap and multi-purpose form of commercial stationery, functioning variously as promotion, street-finder, invoice, business card and compliments slip. They began to appear in London in large numbers in the middle of the eighteenth century, when safety legislation outlawed the projecting shop signs that were widely used by shopkeepers and tradesmen. Without the signs, different strategies were needed to bring customers to the door.

Initially offering little more than a list of names with addresses and trades, they were gradually augmented with product details, prices, terms of business and approving testimonials. Pictures were soon added to the letterpress texts, usually illustrating the products on offer, and rapidly becoming more elaborate and design-conscious, embracing eighteenth-century rococo fashion and fancy typefaces.

In the years before sewers, nightmen were among the unsung heroes of life in most cities, performing their unpleasant (and dangerous) nocturnal duties quietly and anonymously. Their business, essentially the shovelling of the contents of the cesspits of private houses and removing them by cart, was not permitted to begin until after midnight. The illustration to this trade card rather politely places more emphasis on Robert Stone's means of conveyance than on the 'needful edifice' or privy, located at the end of the householder's garden path.

For long regarded as disposable ephemera, trade cards are now recognised as important (but rare) documents of commercial practice and design, and are receiving the avid attention of social historians and students of material culture. The growing collection at London Metropolitan Archives contains over 5,000 such cards and is a significant resource of its kind. **AH, JS**

W. H. Willcox & Co., Ltd.,

ENGINEERS' STORES & MILL FURNISHERS,

34 & 36, SOUTHWARK ST., LONDON.

OFFICES: 23, SOUTHWARK STREET.

Telephone, 737 & 740 Hop.

OIL REFINERY: CASTLE STREET.

ENGINE PACKINGS.

OILS.

WILLCOX'S CYLINDER,
WILLCOX'S LARD,
WILLCOX'S NEATSFOOT,

and Oils of every description.

Telephone, 737 & 740 Hop.

OIL REFINERY: CASTLE STREET.

ENGINE PACKINGS.

OILS.

WILLCOX'S CYLINDER,
WILLCOX'S LARD,
WILLCOX'S NEATSFOOT,

and Oils of every description.

WILLCOX'S **Merchants & Shippers Supplied.** WILLCOX'S CYLINDER OIL

OIL FOR GAS ENGINES

QUOTATIONS AND LISTS ON APPLICATION.

SOLE AGENTS FOR PENBERTHY PATENT INJECTORS.

INDIA-RUBBER SHEET, VALVES AND WASHERS.

"THE WILLCOX" NEW SEMI-ROTARY PATENT PUMP.

ASBESTOS GOODS OF EVERY DESCRIPTION, COTTON WASTE, GAUGE GLASSES, OIL CANS, AND GENERAL ENGINEERS' TOOLS.

LEATHER BELTING MANUFACTURERS.

LON.

a

Buying fire engines

Unfortunately, the vast majority of business archives have not survived to tell the tale of their company's creation, development and contribution to society. Merryweather and Sons, fire engine and fire-fighting equipment manufacturers, is an example of a company whose records were put at risk during a succession of corporate takeovers, a common threat to such material.

The firm was originally established around 1690 by Nathaniel Hadley, a maker of pumps and fire-fighting apparatus. The first fire engine factory was built in 1738. In 1791 Henry Lott joined the firm; he later took over full control, handing it over to his nephew by marriage, Moses Merryweather, when he retired. Moses and his sons continued to manage the business and in 1862 built a new factory in York Street, Lambeth, for the manufacture of steam engines. This closed in 1879, but by then another factory had been built in Greenwich Road. By the end of nineteenth century Merryweather's success had been sealed by their designation as Fire Engine Makers by Appointment to the Royal Family, and they were selling fire-fighting equipment across the world. During the decade before the First World War machines were being distributed as widely as South Africa, Australia, New Zealand, Burma, Egypt, India and China.

Some records generated from this impressive history became part of 'The Merryweather Collection', housed at Fire Service College. Otherwise, two items survive at London Metropolitan Archives. These were donated in 2006 after being rescued from a skip in south Wales, and belonged to the company that had taken over the firm, who in turn had absorbed Merryweather's in the 1980s.

One of the items at LMA is this account book giving detailed information on the supply of new fire engines and repairs to existing equipment, including descriptions, measurements and costs. The ledger also describes the ways in which these often bulky machines were transported. An example is an order fulfilled for the Duke of Devonshire for Chatsworth House: 'two new ship size fire engines for two or four men with metallic pistons & valves wrought iron standards brackets and spindles mounted on iron wheels with copper branch pipes brass nose pipes & two ten feet lengths of rivetted leather pipe to each and painted blue & vermillion complete.'

The long and slow journey of the engines from London to Derbyshire began by boat on the Paddington Canal in December 1831. **RW**

▲ Merryweather and Sons, day book, p. 108
Manuscript on paper, 1830–44
LMA/4516/01/001

The Sun Fire Office worldwide

Fire insurance as a practical, profitable, business was born in the City of London after the Great Fire of London in 1666. The loss of 13,000 buildings focused minds on the cost of rebuilding if disaster struck. The Sun Fire Office (surviving today as Royal and Sun Alliance) started in a modest way in 1706 but by 1800 was a major insurer throughout the United Kingdom and had largely cornered the market in industrial buildings. The next step, once Europe was at peace, was to venture abroad.

The Sun insured in Germany from 1836, but a disastrous fire in Hamburg in 1842 ended the German profits. The company withdrew from foreign adventures and concentrated on gathering as much information as possible about the potential markets and their risks.

The Sun Fire Office archive includes a fascinating and unique series of 309 volumes of memorandum books, containing reports from agents (local merchants or globetrotting Sun employees) between 1837 and 1962 on the potential for providing fire insurance worldwide. The books often act as 'diaries' recording the agents' experiences, with related statistics, hand-drawn plans, printed leaflets, maps, reports, newspaper cuttings and early photographs depicting the places they visited or lived in.

The 1877 volume for Napier, Taranaki, New Zealand, illustrates the wealth of information in these volumes about the growth of towns and the type, structure and condition of their buildings. It contains photographs containing various tantalising views of the new colonial settlement with shops and businesses in the main streets. These images are important: Napier was colonised only twenty years before the photographs were taken, and all the original buildings were levelled by an earthquake in 1931.

The Sun's attitude was one of caution both towards the countries in which they could safely operate and towards the kind of risks which they would insure there. Despite this, they did recognise good prospects in some seemingly unlikely places, and the Sun was one of the first insurance companies to appoint agents in a number of countries around the globe.

In the 1850s the Sun took the plunge, based on their extensive information and risk assessment, appointing agencies in the West Indies, South America, South Africa and the Far East. Agencies opened in Europe, the Ottoman Empire, Japan and the Philippines in the 1860s. Australasia followed and, in the 1880s, the United States. This last step entirely altered the scope of the Sun's business, at home and abroad, and made the company enough money to be able to pay out handsomely (unlike a number of the more local American insurance companies) when the San Francisco earthquake of 1906 razed the city to the ground. **CT**

▼ Sun Fire Office, agent's memorandum book for Napier, Taranaki, New Zealand
Manuscript with photographs, 1877
LMA CLC/B/192/DC/019/ MS35122/187

Karl Marx visits the bootmaker

Peal & Co., bootmakers, produced bespoke footwear for 174 years, between 1791 and 1965. The page depicted here details the order made for Karl Marx (1818–1883), philosopher, political economist and communist revolutionary. Marx spent the last thirty-four years of his life in London, mostly in difficult financial circumstances, with help from friends and supporters. He was just one of Peal's numerous famous customers, who also included Fred Astaire, Theodore Roosevelt and Sir Laurence Olivier, along with many less well-known names, whose footwear requirements are recorded in an aptly titled series of 617 'foot books' in the firm's archives.

In these books the salesmen made measurements and outline drawings of every customer's feet. The volumes were used in the firm's shop and by the travelling salesmen. Entries include particular instructions for each customer order, together with any subsequent details on refits and repairs.

Samuel Peal, a shoemaker from Wirksworth, Derbyshire, moved to east London and founded his business in Stepney Green. He devised, and patented, a technique for rendering clothing materials waterproof by finely brushing them with a coat of India rubber solution known as caoutchouc. The process quickly proved its worth, and Peal's boots and shoes became renowned for their comfort and durability. The success of their products allowed the firm to relocate to the more prestigious West End, and they moved in 1886 to a prime location at 487 Oxford Street. Their international reputation was strengthened through salesmen who, from the 1880s onwards, travelled extensively throughout North and South America, Europe, Asia and the Far East.

These books have an obvious relevance for historians of footwear but are also examples of the kinds of archives that can be used to enthuse younger audiences. They have proved popular in family learning events, at which archives are used to help bring history alive in unexpected ways. Children have enjoyed using the foot books to match up famous people with their footprints, and go on to create drawings, three-dimensional shoe models and footwear fashion shows. **RW**

◀ Peal & Co. Ltd, 'Foot Book' 23
Manuscript on paper, c. 1870–85,
detail of p. 142
LMA 4454/02/003

Brewery archives

This advertisement illustrates the striking visual resources that can be found in business archive collections. A bird's eye view of a re-shaped River Thames is shown with a formidable Black Eagle flying high above, transporting cases of ale and stout. Advertising London and the brand, the Truman brewing company traced its roots back to its founder, Joseph Truman, who acquired the Black Eagle Street brewhouse in Brick Lane from William Bucknall in 1679. Two of Truman's sons, Joseph junior (d. 1733) and Benjamin (d. 1780), continued to develop the business, so that by the late eighteenth century Truman's brewery was the third biggest in London, brewing 60,000 barrels of beer per annum. With a succession of family members and altering ownership of company shares, the name Truman grew in syllables as well as in success and was registered as Truman, Hanbury, Buxton & Co. in 1889. Production reached 400,000 barrels per annum in 1850, making it the largest brewery in London. In 1873 the com-

pany opened a brewery in Burton on Trent, also named the Black Eagle. Truman's became part of Watney Mann in 1972, and the Brick Lane brewery closed in 1988; the building has now been converted into an arts and retail centre.

The Truman collection also includes: documentation recording the process of brewing from stock, bottling and cooperage to gyle books (which record fermentation processes); details of the company's premises, including property deeds and licensing records; papers relating to public houses, including visitation registers, inventories, photographs, sales and deliveries records; and staff records, including wages books and registers of employees. Similarly extensive collections for over twenty brewery archives are held at London Metropolitan Archives, including substantial collections from other important London brewers such as Courage, Watney Combe Reid, Whitbread and Allied Breweries. **RW**

▶ Truman, Hanbury, Buxton & Co.,
advertising poster
c. 1925
LMA B/THB/X/002

MENU

Les Perlières de Whitstable et la Sauce 1936
Les Canapés fin d'Année

La Coupe de Tortue Verte au Vin des Iles
Les Profiteroles au Curry

Le Zéphyr de Sole Auréole

Le Suprême de jeune Poularde Nouvelle Mode
Les Pointes d'Amour fine bouche

La délicieuse Brioche Strasbourgeoise
La Salade aux Œufs d'Or

La Doyenne de Comice Récamier
Les Friandises mon régal

New Year's Eve 1935-36   Cumberland Hotel, London, W.1.

The Lyons Archive

J. Lyons & Co. Ltd, caterers, are best known for the Lyons Corner Houses, which were large restaurants arranged on a number of floors. The first one opened in Coventry Street in 1909, and the chain quickly grew. A successful Corner House might have anything up to 400 staff, serving in differently themed restaurants on separate floors; the ground floor was typically a food hall where produce could be bought to take away, and a range of other services might be offered, including hairdressing, theatre booking and telephone booths.

The firm's hotels were also a major part of their business. Established in 1907, Strand Hotel Ltd opened a suite of gigantic hotels in central and west London, including the Regent Palace Hotel, which at the time of its construction in 1915 was the largest in Europe, with 1,280 rooms. From 1922 Lyons' control over the hotels grew with ownership in shares in the company, and with joint directors of both firms. The firm finally gained full control in 1968, renaming the new subsidiary Strand Hotels Ltd.

The Cumberland Hotel, near Marble Arch, was opened in 1933 with all the mod cons of the time. Alongside the 900 en-suite bedrooms there were extensive facilities with public rooms, restaurants, a grill room and banqueting hall. The menu cards are evidence of the culinary attractions the hotel could offer at times of special celebration. They also allowed their designers some whimsical indulgence, some being three-dimensional and others (such as the horse depicted) having pull-outs (the tongue) to show what would unfold during the proceedings.

The 35 linear shelf metres of Lyons archives date from the late 1880s, when the company was founded, to 1995, when the head office was closed. Besides the management, shareholding, administrative and financial records there is documentation of special company initiatives such as the Lyons Electronic Office (LEO), the first computer in the world capable of use for commercial work, set up in 1954. There are also impressive marketing and advertising series, including hundreds of photographs, films and videos, and press cuttings, advertisements and a set of lithographs, which were commissioned after the Second World War as a way of brightening up Lyons Corner Houses.

The designs of the menus and associated ephemera reflect the aesthetics of their time and can be a source of graphic ideas for advertisers today. They capture the company's vibrant ethos and its success in attracting customers with events and festivities. **RW**

◀◀ ◀ ▼ Lyons & Co. Ltd,
selection of Cumberland Hotel
printed food and drink menus
1936–63
LMA ACC/3527/377

TONIGHT'S RUNNERS

LES HORS D'ŒUVRE LUCULLUS
LES CASSOLETTES DES FRUITS DES TROIS MERS
LE SUPRÊME DE VOLAILLE DERBY
LA SALADE CAPRICE
LES POMMES OLIVETTE
LES FRAMBOISES ROYALE HAWAII
LES FRIANDISES
LE CAFÉ
WINES
Chât. de Selle. Cuvée Spéciale. Provence
Moët & Chandon. Dry Imperial. 1959
Liqueurs

TONIGHT'S RIDERS

ALFRED MARKS
THE SILHOUETTES
TONNY VAN DOMMELIN
TUX
DAGENHAM GIRL PIPERS
*
Dancing to
SYDNEY THOMPSON & HIS BAND
ERIC McDERMOTT & HIS BAND
*
CARLISLE SUITE
CUMBERLAND HOTEL
Saturday, 9th January, 1965

ARIEL HOTEL
*
ALBANY HOTEL
*
REGENT PALACE HOTEL
*
STRAND PALACE HOTEL
*
CUMBERLAND HOTEL

CERTAIN RUNNERS
—*Straight from the horse's mouth!*

TO OPERATE — Slowly bend ... full tongue gently.

PULL

CABARET
*
ROBIN HUNTER
*
JOE McBRIDE
*
THE SILHOUETTES
Produced by
Leslie Roberts
*
THE DAGENHAM
GIRL PIPERS
*
EDDIE STREVENS
and His Band
*
TEDDY
LAWFORD'S
Quintette

NEW YEAR'S EVE
Gala
*
CUMBERLAND
HOTEL
*
1963-64

MENU
Les Natives de Whitstable
au Citron
ou Le Saumon d'Écosse Fumé
ou Le Cocktail de
Crevettes Aurore
—
La Tasse de Tortue Verte
au Vins de Rioja
Les Brindilles Dorées
—
Les Sablettres de Sole
Belle Fin d'Année
—
Le Suprême de Volaille
Grand Éclat
Les Petits Pois Fins
au Beurre
Les Pommes Noisette
—
La Prince
des Fruits Glacés
Nouveau Monde
Les Plaisirs
des Dames
—
Champagne
Heidsieck
Dry Monopole
1955

CHAPTER THREE

LONDON LIFE

The City Corporation's collections record the development of all kinds of organisations and institutions across London, civic and commercial, in their administrative, financial and functional aspects. They make it possible to reconstruct the order of events, to know what happened when, and they invite historians to interpret the why as well as the what. Like all historic collections, they also open all kinds of windows on to everyday life of the past; they contain a huge wealth of information on ordinary people, the conditions in which they lived, the disputes that exercised them, the hardships they had to endure and the pleasures that were available to alleviate them. The great wealth of graphic material, in paintings, prints and photographs, helps further in allowing us to picture the life of earlier generations.

At the most simple biographical level the collections are extraordinarily rich. It has been estimated that half the UK population today is likely to have had at least one ancestor who lived in or passed through London, and if those ancestors are documented at all, the record is likely to be found within the City collections. The archives of the London parishes contain information on the births, marriages and deaths of millions of people, and by combining them with other registers and biographical sources at London Metropolitan Archives it has been possible to develop a project with Ancestry.co.uk to deliver online indexing of 77 million names of past Londoners. The popularity and value of this resource among the ever-growing community of people seeking to trace their family roots is demonstrated through the search statistics for the database, which are also counted in many millions.

Health has always been central to quality of life, and in an age of sophisticated medicine, underpinned by technology and science, it is easy to lose sight of the struggles of the past. The collections include extensive and important holdings in medical history; St Thomas' Hospital, illustrated here, is a particularly significant archive but only one of a number of London hospital archives held at London Metropolitan Archives, including voluntary, special and psychiatric hospitals and a number of workhouse infirmaries. The Nightingale Collection supplements these for anyone pursuing the history of nursing. Unsurprisingly, the collections include many items relating not only to the Great Plague of 1665 but also to other less well-acknowledged but still devastating London epidemics of the past, during which thousands, or even tens of thousands, of people died. All these things have the power to move, but it may be the Foundling Hospital token that brings alive the social realities of the past most poignantly of all.

Crime and punishment have also been important aspects of City life, both for its citizens and for its governors. The Lord Mayor is today the chief magistrate of the City, and for many centuries both he and the City sheriffs had formal responsibilities for the administration of justice. The City Corporation also owns and maintains the Central Criminal Court – the Old Bailey – although the trials that take place there are run by the Crown Court Service. The archives include extensive runs of records from numerous City courts, from the Middle Ages onwards, documenting all kinds of crime, from the petty to the serious. This chapter includes some items focusing on the maintenance of order and the results of wrongdoing: items from the City of London Police archive and its predecessor the City Watch, and representations of prison life. The memorabilia from 7 July 2005 highlight not only that crime is always part of the social fabric but also that the collections are dynamically growing and capture contemporary history as well as that of our ancestors.

London has always been ethnically diverse and the charter of William I (see p. 15) acknowledged the French as well as the English population of the City. The cultural mix has grown hugely over time, and the collections include some important resources in this area; the archives on Jewish life, for example, constitute a major critical mass of materials. In a more contemporary arena the receipt of the Huntley Archives has catalysed the development of London Metropolitan Archives as a centre for the deposit and study of records of the London Afro-Caribbean community.

Life includes relaxation as well as work, and various items are reproduced here to reflect the recreations of Londoners, from the medieval bowls players in the margins of a fourteenth-century Bible to late Victorian circuses. The City Corporation is itself an important sponsor of leisure, through (among other things) its support of parks and green spaces, and the story of Epping Forest is told here through the picturesque memorabilia associated with Queen Victoria's visit in 1882.

Medieval London life

The edges of medieval manuscripts were often viewed by the scribes and limners who worked on them as important spaces for the exercise of the imagination. Sometimes this took the form of simple decorative borders, with floral or abstract themes. In other instances these marginal areas become the location of more sophisticated and fabulous goings-on, where mythical or imaginary creatures are juxtaposed with learned texts and the natural order of things seems to be overturned. And sometimes irreverent characters from medieval life are used more traditionally, as illustrations or amusing vignettes.

This delightful Bible was compiled in England in the early fourteenth century and is heavily decorated throughout with historiated initials and coloured flourishes. The opening folio bears these two separate images: one in the first initial, of a scribe at work (presumably beginning his task of copying this very Bible), and the second, using the coloured border along the bottom margin as a baseline, showing three men engaged in a game of bowls. This is known, from similar illustrations in other manuscripts, to have been a recreation of Londoners since at least the beginning of the thirteenth century, and became so popular by the end of the fourteenth century that laws were brought in prohibiting it, for fear of distracting men from their archery practice. Here the bowls themselves were perhaps playfully prompted by the roundels of the border.

At some point in the fifteenth century the Bible was in the possession of the church of St Peter Cornhill, reputedly the oldest of the City churches (with a legendary foundation date of AD 179), sitting on the site of the original Roman basilica. As well as a grammar school, the church also acquired at this period a separate library building, possibly founded by Hugh Damlett, rector at the church from 1447 to 1476. Damlett was a fellow of Pembroke Hall in Cambridge (and was the Hall's Master 1447–50), while simultaneously known in London as a prominent theologian. He was also a collector of books, as his bequests to numerous institutions (including Guildhall Library) make clear. This Bible was not part of his gift to Guildhall, as a rubric at the end of the main text states that the manuscript belonged to the chantry 'at the altar of the Holy Trinity in the church of St Peter upon Cornhill in London'. It both shows us the kinds of books that City parishes were able to accumulate during the Middle Ages and reminds us of the importance of the church at the centre of parochial life, as a place where such treasures could be housed.

After the Reformation the Bible entered private hands, where it remained until it was bought back by St Peter's Church in the late nineteenth century for £25. It was placed on long-term deposit at Guildhall Library in 1948. **MP**

 ▶ ▼ *Biblia*
Manuscript on vellum, late 13th/early 14th century, illustrative details of fol. 1r
LMA P69/PET1/D/002/MS04158A

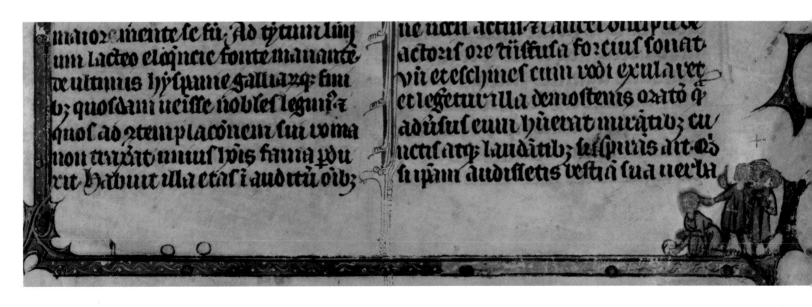

◄ Parish of St Nicholas, Deptford, register of baptisms, marriages and burials (detail showing burial of Christopher Marlowe)
Manuscript on paper, 1563–1796, fol. 145
LMA P78/NIC/001

▼ Parish of St Botolph, Bishopsgate, City of London, register of baptisms, marriages and burials (detail showing baptism of Mary Wollstonecraft)
Manuscript on paper, 1752–79, fol. 66
P69/BOT4/A/003/MS04517/002

Parish records

Documenting the milestones and the regular routines of life at individual and local level, parish archives capture not only births and deaths but also expenditure, office-holding of various kinds, the resolution of disputes and parochial priorities. The parish was a key administrative unit of everyday life, as well as the focus of faith and worship.

During the medieval period parishes mainly documented ecclesiastical affairs and matters relating to the upkeep of their churches and churchyards, but little by way of biographical information. In 1538 Henry VIII's minister Thomas Cromwell issued an order that clergymen must record all baptisms, marriages and burials taking place in their parishes, and the names of those involved. The legislation gradually developed further; Cromwell's injunction was reissued by Edward VI and Elizabeth I, and in 1598 it was ordered that the registers must be kept on parchment. Between the sixteenth and the nineteenth centuries record-keeping further expanded into areas of civil responsibility such as administering poor-law legislation. It is this accumulation of early information that makes parish records invaluable for the study of social, economic, religious and administrative history.

London Metropolitan Archives holds the collections of over 800 parishes, including almost all of the ancient parishes of the diocese of London (excluding the ancient City of

Westminster) and a number for the diocese of Southwark. These parish records date from the medieval period, and great quantities survive, despite the losses suffered during disasters such as the Great Fire of 1666 and the Blitz. The parochial map of London evolved considerably over the centuries; from the seventeenth century onwards, population growth led to the subdivision of many medieval parishes into new ones with their own churches and records, and by the end of the nineteenth century some original parishes had evolved into thirty or forty separate units. As well as the registers of births, marriages and deaths, the records include vestry minutes describing details of community life, rate books providing names of occupiers at particular addresses, and glebe terriers recording church property. Churchwardens' accounts may suggest routine financial transactions but often reveal the unexpected. For example, these sixteenth-century entries for St Botolph, Aldgate, display ornately drawn letters by the curate, Robert Heas.

As anyone who has engaged in genealogical research is aware, parish registers are the primary resource for tracing individuals until civil registration records began in 1837. The countless procession of names includes, every now and then, one that stands out as an historical celebrity: here, for example, is the burial record of the Elizabethan playwright Christopher Marlowe and the baptism entry for the eighteenth-century writer and philosopher Mary Wollstonecraft. But the value of the extraordinary is hugely outweighed by that of the ordinary: with the rise in interest in family history in recent decades, these registers have become the most regularly sought out items in the collections. In 2009 a vast digitisation programme began, in partnership with Ancestry.co.uk, to make the contents of the London parish registers available online. This is transforming the access opportunities and making it easy for people anywhere in the world to quarry the millions and millions of names that they contain. JG

▲ Parish of St Botolph, Aldgate, City of London, Churchwardens' accounts
Manuscript on paper, 1547–85, fols 80, 84
LMA P69/BOT2/B/012/MS09235/001

St Thomas' Hospital

London Metropolitan Archives includes a number of significant collections of London hospitals and other medical institutions. St Thomas' Hospital was founded in Southwark in the twelfth century as a religious institution where patients were cared for by the brothers and sisters. Dissolved by Henry VIII in 1540, it was refounded in 1551 by Henry's son, Edward VI, who granted the hospital to the City of London and in 1553 granted the City lands to support the Royal Hospitals. The patients were now cared for by paid members of staff, whose job descriptions were set out in the Book of the Government of the Hospital, drawn up by Richard Grafton, first Treasurer General of the Royal Hospitals, in 1556.

The matron was to be 'a sadd grave, vertuos, and motherly woman', and she was to have a tender eye for the entertainment and nourishment of the patients. The sisters were instructed to avoid railing, scolding and drunkenness, and to ensure that the wards were kept clean and sweet.

The Book of the Government also sets out the daily allowance of food and drink for the patients. Each patient was to have one 14 oz loaf and three pints of beer every day. On Sundays, Mondays, Tuesdays and Thursdays each group of four patients was to have either 3 lb of beef or a leg or loin of mutton. On Wednesdays, Fridays and Saturdays they had half a pound of butter or a pound of cheese. A double allowance was given on Christmas Day, Shrove Tuesday, Easter and Whitsun.

At this time there were no anaesthetics, no antiseptics and no antibiotics. Treatment in the hospital was limited to the administration of mainly herbal remedies and straightforward surgery such as amputations, which had to be performed as rapidly as possible. Venereal cases were given heat treatment in the four sweat wards at the back of the hospital. **BH**

◀ ▲ St Thomas' Hospital,
Book of the Government
Manuscript on paper, 1556,
fols 27r, 34v
LMA H01/ST/A/024/001

Setting the watch

Written in 1585, this volume records the manner and order of setting the City watch. The phrase 'Watch and Ward', which long described the police system of the City, referred respectively to the night and day guard that was undertaken by the watchmen. The system seems to have been regularised, if not established, by the Statuta Civitatis London of 1285. This was the year in which the Statute of Winchester was enacted, which commanded that watch be kept in all cities and towns, but a separate statute was created to meet the peculiar conditions of the City of London. Originally, every inhabitant of a ward in the City was liable to serve a turn in the watch or to provide a substitute who served under constables chosen to see that the watch was kept. As time went on, the constables began to employ deputies, evading personal service by paying others to do the work for them.

The Statuta provided that the gates of London be shut every night and that the City should be divided into twenty-four wards, each with six watchmen controlled by an alderman. This was known as the 'standing watch' and in times of disturbance was doubled and ordered to be kept day and night. There was also in existence a body called the 'marching watch', to move about and assist the watchmen in the wards. All these watchmen were authorised to arrest offenders and bring them before the Lord Mayor. The system thus established continued for centuries.

In 1737 the nightly watch was reorganised, but no effective daytime police existed in the City until 1784, when Common Council agreed to finance a City patrol as a temporary expedient. However, although small, it was discontinued in 1793 as an unnecessary financial burden. Extra constables were occasionally appointed by the Court of Aldermen as need required. By 1796 they were regularly patrolling the City's streets and soon evolved into a day and a night patrol, numbering sixteen men by 1803 and forty-nine by 1815. The night patrol was disbanded in 1831, and its members transferred into an enlarged day patrol, which, with a new uniform, then became known as the City day police. Policing in the City at night was left to the nightly watch. The following year the Court of Aldermen authorised the expansion of the day police to 100 men, modelled on the ranks, pay and conditions of the recently established Metropolitan Police. It became fully operational in April 1832. In November 1838 an Act of Common Council merged the two City police forces into one, called the Day Police and Nightly Watch, which had a combined establishment of 501 men. By the City of London Police Act, passed in August 1839, the City of London Police, as it now became known, was given statutory approval and pre-empted an attempt to merge the City's police into the Metropolitan Police (see p. 90). **ES**

▶ *The Ancient Manner and Order of Setting the Watch*
Manuscript on paper, 1585, fols 11v–12r
LMA CLA/048/PS/02/001

Plague in London

The City Corporation's collections have many reflections of mortality in earlier generations and of regular anxiety about epidemics. Of all the many diseases that claimed lives, plague had a particular resonance and terror in the popular mind, dating back to the Black Death of the fourteenth century. Plague was visited on early modern London on many occasions. There were major outbreaks in 1563 and 1603, and as many as 35,000 people are thought to have died of plague in 1625. The increase in foreign trade during the period, with opportunities to introduce new carriers of disease, exacerbated the problem.

The virulence and pervasiveness of the epidemic that swept through London in the summer of 1665, which was also the last major outbreak of the disease in England, assured it a permanent place in the popular consciousness and in history. About a fifth of the City's population succumbed, and the authorities were almost overwhelmed. The fact that it was

followed so swiftly by the devastation of the Great Fire meant that the 1660s became a decade of profound and dramatic change for the City.

Acts of Parliament from the reign on Henry VIII onwards had made the parish the fundamental unit of administration for the state. In this capacity parishes were under instructions to keep records of baptisms, marriages and burials (see p. 68). In London the Parish Clerks' Company, not technically a livery company but run on a similar model, began to compile bills of mortality around the same time, comprising weekly lists of deaths with their causes. The published versions of these bills were scrutinised with increasing interest by a fearful public.

The bills for 1665 record the gradual increase and spread of the plague, from its original foothold in St Giles in the Fields throughout the cities of London and Westminster and into the surrounding areas. Deaths reached their peak in the week 12–19 September (see p. 73), when the parish clerks recorded 7,165 deaths from the plague alone, out of a total mortality of 8,297 (pity the poor unnamed souls who, even in such a week, died from 'wind', 'frighted' or 'griefe', or the individual killed by falling from the belfry at All Hallows the Great). The King and his court retreated to Oxfordshire, but the Lord Mayor (Sir John Lawrence) and most of the City aldermen remained at their posts. The Corporation's decision to order a cull of dogs and cats, thought to be spreaders of the disease, was well intended but unfortunate, as cats helped to control the rats whose fleas were the real carriers.

The plague gradually subsided over the rest of September and October, although the epidemic continued to claim victims through the following winter. Burial rates were seven times higher in 1665 than in the previous year. The bills of mortality record nearly 70,000 deaths from the plague in the year, and this figure is almost certainly an under-representation. Many corpses were disposed of without trace, and causes of deaths were often falsified to avoid the stigma of the plague (recorded deaths by other slightly spurious causes rise significantly in the period). The scale of the devastation soon led to its common appellation, the 'Great Plague', almost obliterating previous epidemics from memory and putting its reputation on a par only with the Black Death some three hundred years earlier.

The bills of mortality continued to be compiled until 1858, when the arrangements for civil registration of deaths finally made them redundant. MP

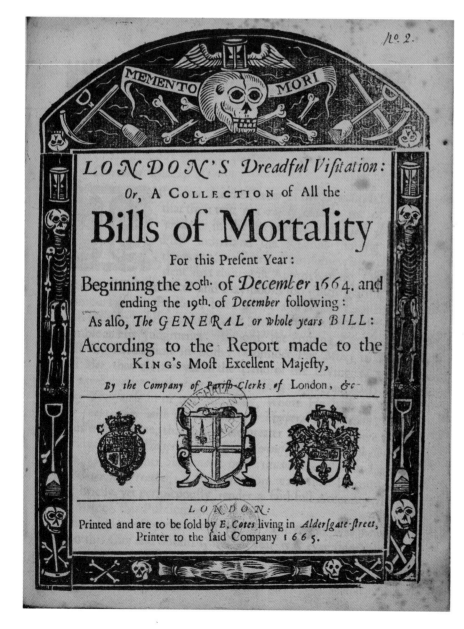

◀ *London's Dreadful Visitation: or,*
A Collection of All the Bills of Mortality
Printed in London, 1665, title page
GHL A.1.5 no.2

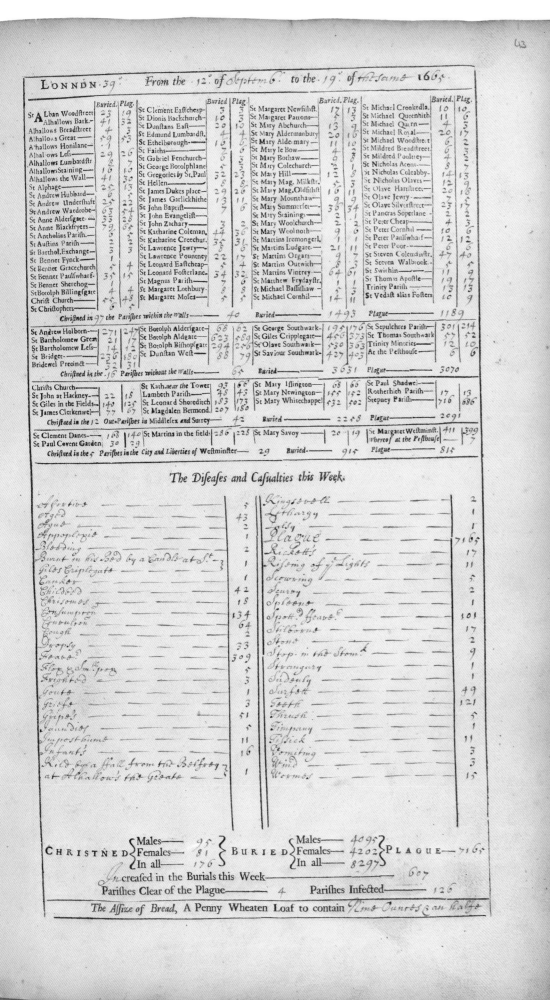

Worshipful Company of Parish Clerks, bills of mortality
Print and manuscript on paper, 12–19 September 1665, fol. 43
LMA CLC/L/PB/E/001A/ MS03604/001/001

LONDON 39. From the 12° of September to the 19° of the same 1665.

Parish	Buried	Plag.
St Alban Woodstreet	23	19
Alhallows Bark.	41	32
Alhallows Breadstreet	4	3
Alhallows Great	59	53
Alhallows Honilane	1	1
Alhallows Less	29	26
Alhallows Lumbardstr	8	7
Alhallows Staining	16	10
Alhallows the Wall	41	30
St Alphage	25	13
St Andrew Hubbard	6	5
St Andrew Undershaft	25	22
St Andrew Wardrobe	63	54
St Anne Aldersgate	33	30
St Anne Blackfryers	79	65
St Antholins Parish	2	2
St Austins Parish	2	2
St Barthol. Exchange	3	3
St Bennet Fynck		
St Bennet Gracechurch	5	4
St Bennet Paulswharf	35	15
St Bennet Sherehog		
St Botolph Billingsgate	4	4
Christ Church	55	48
St Christophers	6	5

Parish	Buried	Plag.
St Clement Eastcheap	3	3
St Dionis Backchurch	10	3
St Dunstans East	20	10
St Edmund Lumbardst.	4	4
St Ethelborough	6	6
St Faiths	6	6
St Gabriel Fenchurch	6	3
St George Botolphlane	4	4
St Gregories by St Paul	32	23
St Hellen		
St James Dukes place	29	26
St James Garlickhithe	13	11
St John Baptist	7	6
St John Evangelist		
St John Zachary	5	5
St Katharine Coleman	44	36
St Katharine Creechur.	35	31
St Lawrence Jewry		
St Lawrence Pountney	22	17
St Leonard Eastcheap	5	4
St Leonard Fosterlane	34	32
St Magnus Parish	7	5
St Margaret Lothbury	8	8
St Margaret Moses	5	5

Parish	Buried	Plag.
St Margaret Newfishst	17	13
St Margaret Patons	7	5
St Mary Abchurch	13	9
St Mary Aldermanbury	20	16
St Mary Aldermary	11	10
St Mary le Bow	4	4
St Mary Bothaw	4	4
St Mary Colechurch		
St Mary Hill	12	8
St Mary Mag. Milkstr		
St Mary Mag. Oldfishst	16	11
St Mary Mounthaw	9	9
St Mary Summerset	36	34
St Mary Stainings	2	2
St Mary Woolchurch	3	2
St Mary Woolnoth	9	6
St Martins Ironmongerl.	1	1
St Martins Ludgate	21	11
St Martins Orgars	9	7
St Martins Outwich	8	3
St Martins Vintrey	64	61
St Matthew Frydaystr.	1	1
St Michael Bassishaw	5	3
St Michael Cornhil	14	11

Parish	Buried	Plag.
St Michael Crookedla.	10	10
St Michael Queenhith	11	6
St Michael Quern	4	3
St Michael Royal	20	17
St Michael Woodstreet	6	6
St Mildred Breadstreet	6	6
St Mildred Poultrey	4	4
St Nicholas Acons		
St Nicholas Coleabby	14	13
St Nicholas Olaves	12	9
St Olave Hartstreet	20	18
St Olave Jewry		
St Olave Silverstreet	23	17
St Pancras Soperlane	2	2
St Peter Cheap	4	3
St Peter Cornhil	10	6
St Peter Paulswharf	12	12
St Peter Poor	6	6
St Steven Colemanstr.	47	40
St Steven Walbrook	5	5
St Swithin	11	9
St Thomas Apostle	19	17
Trinity Parish	13	13
St Vedast alias Fosters	10	9

Christned in 97 the Parishes within the walls — 40   Buried — 1493   Plague — 1189

Parish	Buried	Plag.
St Andrew Holborn	271	247
St Bartholomew Great	21	17
St Bartholomew Less	14	12
St Bridget	236	190
Bridewell Precinct	52	31

Parish	Buried	Plag.
St Botolph Aldersgate	68	62
St Botolph Aldgate	623	589
St Botolph Bishopsgate	294	256
St Dunstan West	88	79

Parish	Buried	Plag.
St George Southwark	195	176
St Giles Cripplegate	456	373
St Olave Southwark	530	363
St Saviour Southwark	427	403

Parish	Buried	Plag.
St Sepulchres Parish	301	214
St Thomas Southwark	57	52
Trinity Minories	12	10
At the Pesthouse	6	6

Christned in the 16 Parishes without the walls — 64   Buried — 3631   Plague — 3070

Parish	Buried	Plag.
Christs Church		
St John at Hackney	22	18
St Giles in the Fields	140	125
St James Clerkenwel	77	67

Parish	Buried	Plag.
St Kath. near the Tower	93	66
Lambeth Parish	48	43
St Leonard Shoreditch	183	173
St Magdalen Bermond.	207	180

Parish	Buried	Plag.
St Mary Islington	68	66
St Mary Newington	155	152
St Mary Whitechappel	532	502

Parish	Buried	Plag.
St Paul Shadwel		
Rotherhith Parish	17	13
Stepney Parish	716	686

Christned in the 12 Out-Parishes in Middlesex and Surrey — 42   Buried — 2248   Plague — 2091

Parish	Buried	Plag.
St Clement Danes	168	140
St Paul Covent Garden	30	29

Parish	Buried	Plag.
St Martins in the fields	286	228

Parish	Buried	Plag.
St Mary Savoy	20	19

Parish	Buried	Plag.
St Margaret Westminst.	411	399
Whereof at the Pesthouse		7

Christned in the 5 Parishes in the City and Liberties of Westminster — 29   Buried — 915   Plague — 815

The Diseases and Casualties this Week.

Abortive	5
Aged	43
Ague	2
Appoplexie	1
Bleeding	2
Burnt in his Bed by a Candle at St. Giles Cripplegate	1
Canker	
Childbed	42
Chrisomes	18
Consumption	134
Convulsion	64
Cough	2
Dropsy	33
Feaver	309
Flox & small Pox	5
Frighted	3
Gout	1
Grief	3
Griping	51
Jaundies	5
Imposthume	11
Infants	16
Kild by a fall from the Belfry at Alhallow's the Greate	1

Kingsevill	2
Lethargy	1
Palsy	1
Plague	7165
Rickets	17
Rising of the Lights	11
Scowring	5
Scurvy	2
Spleene	1
Spotted Feaver	101
Stilborne	17
Stone	2
Stop. in the Stomak	9
Strangury	1
Suddenly	
Surfeit	49
Teeth	121
Thrush	5
Timpany	1
Tissick	11
Vomiting	3
Wind	3
Wormes	15

Christned { Males — 95 { Females — 81 { In all — 176   Buried { Males — 4095 { Females — 4202 { In all — 8297   Plague — 7165

Increased in the Burials this Week — 607

Parishes Clear of the Plague — 4   Parishes Infected — 126

The Assize of Bread, A Penny Wheaten Loaf to contain Nine Ounces and a half.

The Foundling Hospital

This small scrap of cloth, with some unaccomplished needle-work embroidered on it, hardly looks much but is, perhaps, among the most moving and personal artefacts to be found among the archive collections. The billet books of the Foundling Hospital include the small tokens that were all that desperate mothers could leave with their babies when they had to abandon them to institutional care.

In post-Reformation London, Christ's Hospital had taken over some of the functions of the dissolved monasteries by taking in unwanted children. From 1676 it decided to accept only legitimate children, so unmarried mothers were forced to seek help from their parishes. The population explosion of London at this time put increased pressure on parochial resources, while people's mobility made it increasingly difficult to track who was responsible for whom.

In 1739 Thomas Coram was granted a royal charter to set up the Foundling Hospital in order to alleviate the problem. Children of less than two months old were accepted, baptised and then boarded out to a wet or dry nurse (a dry nurse bottle-fed the baby). When the child was three years old, it would be returned to the Foundling Hospital at its premises in Bloomsbury, where it would be educated until it was apprenticed, placed in service or enrolled in the armed forces.

Originally admission was operated on a 'first come, first served' basis, but as the massive demand for places became obvious, a ballot system was introduced. Women bringing a child to the hospital would draw a ball out of a bag. If the ball was black, their child was rejected; if the ball was white, their child would be subject to an inspection and, if found to be healthy, would be accepted. Women who drew a red ball would have their children accepted if any of the white-ball babies were rejected. This became something of spectator sport; an engraving by Samuel Wale from 1749 shows fashionable ladies ogling the poor unfortunate mothers taking part in the ballot.

When a child was accepted by the hospital, an inventory was taken of its clothes. These registers also contain small tokens that mothers left with their children. Some composed poems, while others spent their precious pennies on a piece of ribbon or a small toy. The mother of this six-week-old baby girl took the time to stitch a small strip of linen, perhaps to remind her baby that her mother cared for her, or perhaps even as a reminder of the name that her mother had given her before she was baptised by the hospital. She probably never saw her child again. **JV**

▶ ▼ The Foundling Hospital, billet book
Manuscript and print on paper, and fabric, 1756, fol. 1366, and associated tokens
LMA A/FH/A/09/001/018

Frost fairs

Although we think our winters can be cold, we should reflect not only on the realities of life before central heating but also on the harshness of London winters between the fourteenth century and the nineteenth, a period that climate historians have called the Little Ice Age. Temperatures dropped and stayed low for long periods, and the Thames often froze over. The thick piers of Old London Bridge, before their demolition in 1832, impeded water flow and made it easier for ice to form. When the ice was thick enough, traders and entertainers of all kinds ventured out and created frost fairs, which could last for weeks. The first such fair was recorded in 1608 and the last in 1814, when an elephant was reputedly led across the ice below Blackfriars Bridge.

A severe frost began on Christmas Day 1739, which continued until February, with the result that the Thames soon froze so solidly that tents and booths were erected on the ice. On 31 January 1740 the *Gentleman's Magazine* recorded that 'The Thames floated with rocks and shoals of Ice; rising everywhere in hillocks and huge Rocks of Ice and Snow; of which Scene several Painters took Sketches. Booths, Stalls and Printing-Presses were erected, and a Frost-Fair held on it.' Booths were erected to sell toys and millinery, and there was even a printing press erected to produce souvenirs; William Hogarth had a ticket printed for Trump, his dog. Other entertainments held on the ice included bear-baiting, cat-throwing and 'flying roundabouts'.

Unfortunately the ice was not completely safe. The *Gentleman's Magazine* account also notes that 'Multitudes walk'd over it, and some were lost by their Rashness.' Added to this loss of life above London Bridge, a considerable amount of damage was done below the bridge when a severe gale, combined with the ice, caused £100,000 worth of destruction and further loss of life between the City and the Medway.

Jan Griffier's view of this particularly elaborate fair is taken from near Whitehall and extends north and east from Westminster Bridge on the right (then under construction). St Paul's Cathedral is in the distance, with the Monument and the Tower of London in the centre. **NA, JJ**

▶▶ Jan Griffier, *The Thames during the Great Frost of 1739*
Oil on canvas, 1739
GAG 1706

FOUNDLING HOSPITAL, 8th May 1756 at 11½ o'Clock

Letter B a Female Child about 5 weeks old

N.o 1366

I'm sent to find,
If Fortunes kind,
And should it now prove true,
My Parent fond,
Will not Despond,
Of Sarah Montague.

a Mark
Resembling a Scar
on ye forehead
& small red speck
between the Eyes.
May. 8. 1756

Frock
Upper-Coat
Petticoat
Bodice-Coat
Barrow
Mantle
Sleeves
Blanket
Neckcloth
Roller
Bed
Waistcoat
Shirt
Clout
Pilch
Stockings
Shoes

Marks on the Body.

with the inclosed paper

Crime and punishment

The City has always been a place for the administration of justice and the punishment of malefactors. In the early Middle Ages the Court of Hustings dealt with disputes between citizens, and from the thirteenth century onwards a Mayor's Court existed to deal with an ever-growing amount of litigation. The City sheriffs also had their own courts, and specialist courts for Requests (small debts) and Orphans (to supervise estate administration of orphaned freemen's sons) were also set up. The Guildhall was sometimes used as a place for high-profile trials; Lady Jane Grey and Archbishop Thomas Cranmer were tried there in the 1550s and Henry Garnet, the Jesuit priest executed for complicity in the Gunpowder Plot, in 1606. The City Corporation's archives hold extensive documentation of many centuries' worth of legal cases; most of them are relatively trivial, but they all cast a light on the realities of past lives.

The collections include not only the records of many courts over the years but also more graphic depictions of the ways in which criminals were treated. Measures that we now regard as barbaric and inhumane were commonplace for many centuries. The barbarity of prison life in the late seventeenth century was shown in Moses Pitt's *Cry of the Oppressed*, which describes the cruelties of contemporary debtors' prisons; some inmates were 'not only iron'd, and lodg'd with hogs, felons, and condemn'd persons, but have had their bones broke; others poisoned and starved to death'. Pitt was a bookseller with direct personal experience of prison life, having been twice jailed for debt. His illustrated text made a strong case for reform, but that was some years off; imprisonment for debt continued until 1870.

The City has had numerous prisons within its boundaries. Compters – jails for petty criminals – were established at various times in Bread Street, Giltspur Street, Poultry and Wood Street, and the City gatehouses were often used as places of incarceration. The Tun, a two-storey barrel-shaped building in Cornhill, was built in 1282 by the mayor, Henry de Waleis, as a lock-up for anyone caught breaking the City curfew. The most notorious and long-lasting of the City prisons was Newgate, which for many centuries was a preoccupation for London's chroniclers and artists as a place of horror, filth and disease.

Newgate jail stood just within the City boundary, on the site of what is now the Central Criminal Court (the Old Bailey); first built in 1188, it was one of London's main prisons and places of execution until it was demolished in 1904. It was substantially rebuilt in 1423, as one of the benefactions from Richard Whittington's estate (see p. 26), and again after the Great Fire in 1666. James Boswell, after a visit there in the 1760s, found it difficult to proceed with the rest of his day's activities, 'Newgate being upon my mind like a black cloud'. The Corporation's archives include the plans for its complete rebuilding in 1770–78, by George Dance the Younger. Although architecturally more distinguished, the new prison did little to improve the sufferings of the inmates, or to change the strange fascination that the place exerted on the minds of Londoners.

The celebrated Victorian artist Gustave Doré was born in France and worked as a literary illustrator there before beginning to work for British publishers in the 1850s. His

▲ Moses Pitt, *The Cry of the Oppressed*
Printed in London, 1691, plate facing p. 7
GHL A.1.1 no.79

illustrated English Bible (1866) was a great success, leading to an exhibition in London the following year, which raised his profile with British audiences. In 1869 he was commissioned to undertake a pictorial overview of London, which resulted in *London: A Pilgrimage*, published in 1872. Its 174 wood-engravings, many of which focus on the poverty and hardship of much of the urban life of the time, have become well-known images of the Victorian city.

The dark and brooding style that often characterises Doré's work was aptly applied to Newgate, where his image of the exercise yard conjures up the bleakness and sense of futility that agitated prison reformers. Vincent Van Gogh, an ardent admirer of Victorian book and periodical illustration, who saw this picture in 1890, was inspired to create his own painting of bleakly circling prisoners (now in the Pushkin Museum of Fine Arts, Moscow). JS

◄ Blanchard Jerrold and Gustave Doré, *London: A Pilgrimage*
Printed in London, 1872, plate facing p. 136
GHL GR 2.3.6

Coffee house culture

Coffee, as a drink, was popular in the Middle East before spreading to Europe in the seventeenth century. The first coffee house in the City was established on Cornhill in 1652, quickly followed by many others. They developed an important role as places of both recreation and commerce; Lloyd's insurance business, for example, began life in a coffee house (see p. 56), along with the share-trading that became the Stock Exchange (see p. 52).

In this picture a group of stockjobbers is mixing business with pleasure, perhaps in Garraway's Coffee House in Exchange Alley, Cornhill, which was famed for its punch and sherry. Established in 1669, Garraway's developed from a place to trade in fur and ships to a business hub for other products, including tea, coffee, sugar, spices, textiles and salvaged goods. It also became an important base for auction sales.

Stockjobbers operated in a murky world between businesses and their shareholders, and were generally held in low account. In 1696 Parliament set up an enquiry into the 'pernicious art of stock jobbing' in response to some of their notorious activities. The resulting legislation aimed at restraining them by ensuring they were licensed by the City Corporation, approved and registered by the Lord Mayor and the Court of Aldermen.

Although he was self-styled as a 'drawing master' when his work first appeared at the Royal Academy in 1774, much of Robert Dighton's activity was centred on caricature drawings. He drew illustrations of actors for John Bell's edition of Shakespeare in the 1770s and was an actor and singer himself, appearing variously at Covent Garden, the Haymarket and Sadler's Wells. In 1806 he was caught stealing prints from the British Museum; by offering to draw portraits of museum officials he gained access to the collections so as to be able to pilfer them. Had he not then sold them on the London art market, he might have got away with it. **NA, JJ**

The lottery

▲ Robert Dighton, *Stock-jobbers Extraordinary*
Watercolour on paper, c. 1795
GAG 1255

▶ *On State Lottery's*
Engraving on paper, published by I. Carwitham, 1739
LMA SC/GL/PR/281/GUI/INT

The National Lottery is a familiar part of our social landscape but is a recent creation, started in 1994. State-run lotteries have a long history in English life, however, as the first known one was run in 1569 and drawn in St Paul's Churchyard. Like today's lottery, it was established to fund good causes and public works, with 40,000 'chances' sold at 10 shillings each. Both public and private lotteries continued thereafter in Britain, often allied to particular projects; in the American colonies the settlement of Virginia in the seventeenth century and the founding of Princeton and Columbia universities in the eighteenth were part-funded by lottery receipts.

For much of the eighteenth century, the English state lottery, which ran between 1694 and 1826, was drawn in Guildhall, where this depiction is set. The president of the lottery board, with his deputies and clerks, presides on the rostrum while boys from the nearby Blue Coat School (who were evidently regarded as trustworthy) prepare to make the draw. One lottery wheel contains the tickets and the other the certificates naming the prizes (or if unlucky, a blank). Both wheels were spun, and the prize and the prizewinner would be matched. The windfall often consisted of property (land or buildings) rather than money or bonds.

Lottery tickets could involve a substantial investment – in the eighteenth century, tickets might be £10 apiece – and often syndicates would be formed with certificates to record each contribution or stake. Licensed outlets, run as competitive commercial concerns, issued the actual tickets along with prospectuses and other promotional literature. All this activity, then as now, generated a range of ephemera, and this print is part of an extensive collection of such material now held at Guildhall Library and London Metropolitan Archives.

Lotteries created opportunities for frauds and scams and were politically controversial. In October 1826 the announcement was made that 'all lotteries will end forever', and the state withdrew from this kind of fund raising until its revival in 1994. **JS**

ON STATE LOTTERYS.

The Name of a LOTT'RY the Nation bewitches, | The Footman resolves, if he meets no Disaster,
And City and Country run Mad after Riches: | To mount his gilt Chariot, and vie with his Master:
My Lord, who already has Thousands a Year, | The Cook-Wench determines, by one lucky Hit,
Thinks to double his Income by vent'ring it there: | To free her fair Hands from the Pot-hooks and Spit:
The Country Squire dips his Houses and Grounds, | The Chamber-maid Struts in her Ladies Cast Gown,
For Tickets to gain him the Ten Thousand Pounds: | And hopes to be dub'd the Top Toast of the Town:
The rosie-jowl'd Doctor his Rectorie leaves, | But Fortune alass! will have small Share of Thanks,
In quest of a Prize, to procure him Lawn-Sleeves | When all their high Wishes are bury'd in Blanks:
The Tradesman, whom Duns for their Mony importune | For tho' they for Benefits eagerly watch'd,
Here, hazards his All, for th'Advance of his Fortune: | They reckon'd their Chickens before they were hatch'd.

Sold by I. Carwitham Engraver in King street St Giles's.

Jewish life

London Metropolitan Archives holds one of the most important collections of Jewish archives in the country. Its collections relating to the history of Jewish life in London are unrivalled, as the archives of major nationwide Jewish organisations, all based in London, have been deposited there, as have those of many schools, synagogues and charities working in London for the local Jewish population.

Jewish communities have been continuously resident in London since their re-admission to England by Oliver Cromwell in the 1650s; they had previously been expelled by Edward I in 1290. The first new synagogues to be built in London in the seventeenth century were based around Aldgate, in the City of London, and the focus of Jewish settlement remained in the City and the East End until the mid-twentieth century.

In the years after 1881 the Jewish population of the East End of London expanded considerably as refugees from eastern Europe arrived in their thousands. The newcomers were able to benefit from a familiar cultural and religious environment, and from charitable, religious and social support networks that were already well established. Many of the organisations providing this support have deposited their archive collections with the City. Large institutions with a national remit, such as the Office of the Chief Rabbi, the Board of Deputies of British Jews and the Beth Din (the court of the Chief Rabbi), are included, as are national and international welfare organisations, including World Jewish Relief. Education is also well represented, especially through the archive of the Jews' Free School (now JFS Comprehensive). Local charitable organisations range from the Jewish Memorial Council, a major educational charity based in Bloomsbury, to the tiny Soup Kitchen for the Jewish Poor in Stepney.

The archives of religious congregations span all branches of Judaism, both Ashkenazi (Jews from eastern Europe) and Sephardi (from Spain and Portugal), and from orthodox to liberal, including the orthodox United Synagogue, the liberal Jewish Synagogue and the Spanish and Portuguese Jews' Congregation. The last of these was the first community to return to England in the seventeenth century, worshipping first in a small synagogue in Creechurch Lane in the City of London. As the congregation grew, so did the need for a bigger place of worship. In 1699 a committee consisting of members of the congregation hired Joseph Avis, a Quaker, to build the new synagogue and leased land for the purpose in Bevis Marks, tucked away in a back street in the City (Jews were still not allowed to build on the public highway). In 1747 a member of the community, Benjamin Mendes da Costa, bought the lease of the ground on which the synagogue stood and presented it to the congregation. Bevis Marks Synagogue opened in 1702 and is still in use today, the oldest working synagogue in England.

The Spanish and Portuguese Jews' Congregation used a burial ground in Mile End Road, east London (now known as the 'Velho', or 'Old', Cemetery), but by 1720 there was little space left in this cemetery. The Congregation therefore negotiated the purchase of 2½ acres of extra land further east along Mile End Road, to guard against the day when a new cemetery was required. The 'Novo' ('New') Cemetery was brought into use in 1733, paid for by wealthy members of the congregation, who put their names and seals to an indenture for the purpose in 1734. The Novo Cemetery was extended by an additional 4½ acres in 1849.

The congregation continued to expand and began to move out of the City and East End of London during the nineteenth century. In 1896 its new synagogue was built in Maida Vale, west London. **NiA**

◀ The interior of Bevis Marks Synagogue, looking towards the entrance
Photographic print, 1968
LMA SC/PHL/01/1219/68/06949

▶ Indenture relating to the acquisition of the 'Novo' Cemetery in Mile End Road (detail)
Manuscript on parchment,
14 February 1734
LMA 4521/A/03/02/001

Travelling to Brighton in 1831

Looking east towards the tower of St Mary-Le-Bow, this picture captures a typical scene in Cheapside, one of the key thoroughfares in the City, in the early nineteenth century. It shows a bustling street filled with pedestrians, carriages and coaches, with the London–Brighton stage coach (in the centre of the painting) ready to begin its journey.

Cheapside as a flourishing area of commerce and retailing has a long history, beginning in medieval London as the City's chief marketplace, with each guild established in nearby areas and streets. By the 1720s Cheapside was described as 'a spacious street adorned with lofty buildings', and during the mid-nineteenth century it could rival the West End as a major shopping centre. Although its profile in this sense declined during the twentieth century, the opening of the new shopping complex at One New Change in 2010 is again drawing retailers and shoppers back into the City.

Cheapside has been the venue for many notable events and processions. Its fountains flowed with wine to celebrate medieval coronations, and punishments or executions took place there, in the stocks or next to the 'Standard' fountain. Many famous people have had links with Cheapside: Thomas Becket was born in a house on the corner of Ironmonger Lane; Sir Christopher Wren rebuilt St Mary-le-Bow following the Great Fire; and John Keats lived in a house opposite Ironmonger Lane.

The stage coach was introduced to London as early as the 1640s, and soon became the main means of transport to major cities. By the end of the eighteenth century it was also regularly being used for shorter journeys. As the nineteenth century progressed, the volume of traffic increased and congestion became a growing problem; hackney carriages jostled alongside the larger stage coaches, and omnibuses began to appear on the streets in 1829 (see p. 116).

The itinerant English artist William Turner de Lond's attention to detail, both generally and topographically, led him to develop a particular expertise in the genre of busy street scenes and bustling city life. Although better known for his views of the city of Edinburgh, particularly the burning of the Old Town in 1824, Turner de Lond also painted in London and Ireland. He was able to record the visits of George IV both to Dublin in 1821 and to Edinburgh in 1822. Returning to Ireland in later life, in 1837 he again painted an image of destruction: that of the Royal Arcade in Dublin, following a major fire. 'De Lond', as he signed his works, was sometimes mistaken by contemporaries for the far more famous landscape painter J. M. W. Turner. **JJ**

◀ William Turner de Lond,
The London to Brighton Coach at Cheapside
Oil on panel, 1831
GAG 4190

Barrack Hospital
Scutari
Septr 6th
1855.

Mrs Hunt,

I grieve to be obliged to inform you that your son died in this Hospital on Sunday last, Septr 2d. His complaint was Chronic Dysentery — he sunk gradually from

weakness, without much suffering. Every thing was done that was possible to keep up his strength. He was fed every half hour with the most nourishing things he could take, & when there was any thing he had a fancy for it was taken to him immediately. He sometimes asked for Oranges & Grapes, which quenched his thirst, & which he had, whenever he wished for them —

The Lady with the Lamp

The City Corporation's extensive collections of interest to medical and social historians include a major body of material relating to Florence Nightingale, the 'Lady with the Lamp', who helped to transform nursing during the nineteenth century. The archives of the Nightingale School and the Nightingale Collection of correspondence, prints, photographs, publications and manuscripts, now owned by the Florence Nightingale Museum Trust, are deposited in London Metropolitan Archives. Many of the letters written by and to Nightingale concern either the reform of nursing or the Crimean War.

Florence Nightingale was born into a wealthy family in 1820. Highly intelligent, she was given an unusually thorough education by her father, studying mathematics, constitutional history, Greek, Latin and modern languages. As she grew older, she became increasingly frustrated with the stultifying social round to which the lives of upper-class women were restricted. She felt called by God to nurse the sick. After years of opposition, in 1851 her parents agreed that she should spend three months training at a hospital at Kaiserswerth in Germany. In 1853 she became superintendent of a hospital for invalid gentlewomen in Harley Street.

The following year the Crimean War broke out. Reports in *The Times* exposed the appalling neglect suffered by sick and wounded British soldiers, who had only male orderlies to care for them, whereas French soldiers were nursed by Catholic nuns. In response to the public outcry the government asked Florence Nightingale to lead a party of female nurses to the military hospitals at Scutari. Her success not only in nursing the sick but also in exposing and remedying the insanitary state of the hospitals made her a national heroine. As an old soldier wrote to her many years later: 'That was dreadful times at the Hospital where so many sick and wounded comrades died, a sight I shall ever remember, when God sent you as a Angel of Mercy amongst us.' In the letter

...e spoke much of his Mother, [&] gave us the direction to [you] in his last moments. [He] was very desirous that [you] should be written to about him. His great anxiety [was] that his Mother should receive the pay due to him, & should know that he had not received any pay since he had been out, which he wished his friends to be told that they might apply to the War office for the whole of the pay due to him. He was very

grateful for whatever was done for him, & very patient. You may have the satisfaction of knowing that he had the most constant & careful attendance from the Doctors & the Nurses of the Hospital. The Chaplain & myself saw him every day. He died very peacefully. & sorrowful as this news is for his bereaved Mother. May she find comfort in thinking that his earthly sufferings are over, & in the hope that our Almighty Father will receive him into better world through the blessed promises of our Lord. With sincere sympathy I am yours truly,

Florence Nightingale

illustrated Nightingale tells Mrs Hunt of her son's death from chronic dysentery.

Florence Nightingale shrank from publicity, and on her return to Britain after the war she led a secluded life while continuing to work for the reform of army conditions. She also turned her attention to the sanitary state of India, the care of the sick in the metropolitan workhouses, the introduction of trained professional nursing to hospitals and the development of district nursing. In 1855 her friends and family started a charitable appeal, the Nightingale Fund, to raise money to found a training school for nurses. This opened at St Thomas' Hospital in June 1860, and the influence of nurses from the Nightingale Training School gradually spread all over the world.

In her final years Nightingale was honoured with the Order of Merit (1907) and the Honorary Freedom of the City of London (1908). She died, aged ninety, in 1910. **BH**

▲ Florence Nightingale,
letter to a soldier's mother
Manuscript on paper,
6 September 1855
LMA H01/ST/NC/01/55/4

▶ E. Walker (after a drawing
by W. Simpson), *Florence
Nightingale in a Ward in the
Barrack Hospital at Scutari*
(detail)
Lithograph on paper, 1855
LMA H01/ST/NCPH/A/I/001

CHINGFORD OLD CHURCH

JUSTICE

NEAR Qⁿ ELIZABETH'S LODGE

Getting out and about

Although the City Corporation is widely recognised as the guardian of the Square Mile itself, with its parks and gardens, it is less well known that other important green spaces around outer London are also in its custody, and maintained by the Corporation for public benefit. It owns and cares for over 10,000 acres of public spaces, including Hampstead Heath, Burnham Beeches, West Ham Park and Epping Forest. The basis of this philanthropy dates back to the late nineteenth century, when the Corporation began to react to the way in which the expansion of suburban London was swallowing up huge tracts of open land.

Epping Forest's survival as an open space is largely the result of radical legal action instigated by the City in 1871. Formerly part of the royal forest of Waltham, much of Epping's woodland had been enclosed or developed for farm-land by the middle of the nineteenth century. Through purchase of a small piece of land in Little Ilford in 1854 (later the City of London Cemetery) the Corporation acquired commoners' rights in the Forest. It then used these to fight a test case in the Court of Chancery on behalf of all common-ers of Epping Forest, to prevent further enclosure of land and allow reclamation of land already enclosed.

After three years and considerable expense the Master of the Rolls decided in the City's favour. The Lord Mayor and sheriffs, accompanied by nearly 700 guests, made a formal visit to the Forest in October 1875 to celebrate the achieve-ment. A special train was organised to transfer visitors from Liverpool Street to Snaresbrook; a railway pass for this journey (illustrated opposite) was attached to the commem-orative invitation.

In 1878, after further work to decide how Epping Forest should be disafforested and managed, two groundbreaking Acts of Parliament were passed. These granted the City of London Corporation the right to acquire and protect both Epping Forest and land within 25 miles of the City for the recreation and enjoyment of the public. These acts are of major significance not only as the victory of the common man over the lords of the manor but also because they enshrine in law the notion that people have a right of access to open space regardless of where they live. This concept pro-vided inspiration for later green-belt policies to protect natural and semi-natural environments around British cities from overdevelopment.

The battle finally won, a special visit to Epping Forest by Queen Victoria was organised in May 1882, and the second beautiful and highly decorative invitation shown opposite was produced. The Queen was conveyed by train from Windsor to Chingford and then by carriage to a scenic part of the forest, where a special amphitheatre was erected for 2,000 spectators. The Lord Mayor gave an address, and the Queen declared that 'It gives me the greatest satisfaction to dedicate this beautiful forest to the use and enjoyment of my people for all time.' Epping Forest's 6,000 acres, the largest publicly owned space in the London area, have been looked after by the City Corporation ever since. They include a hunting lodge, now known as Queen Elizabeth's Hunting Lodge but actually built for Henry VIII in 1543, and Wanstead Park, the land-scaped grounds of the long-demolished Wanstead House. **KK**

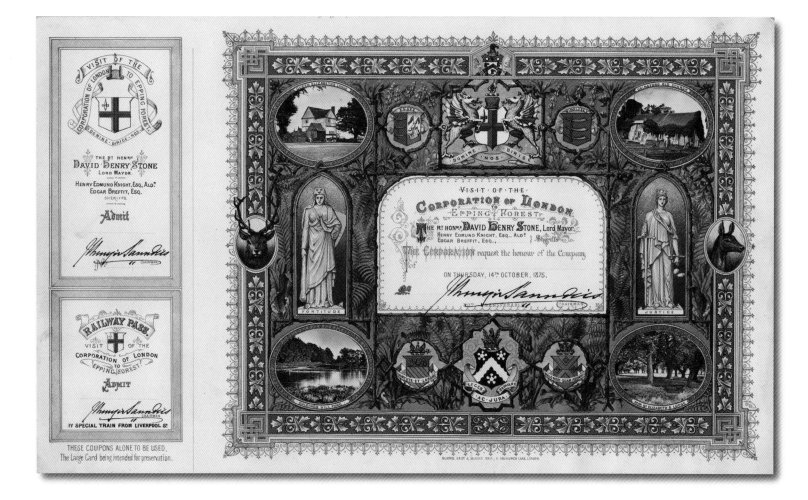

◀ ▲ Invitation with attached ticket and train pass for visit of the Corporation of London to Epping Forest
Chromolithograph with inset Woodburytype photographs, 1875
SL/GL/CIV 1875

▶ Invitation for the visit of Queen Victoria to Epping Forest
Chromolithograph, 1882
LMA CLA/077/F/04/002/B

The boys in blue

In 1839 a Parliamentary act 'for regulating the Police in the City of London', sponsored by the Corporation, established the City of London Police as a separate force from the Metropolitan Police. Most of the archive relating to the City Police, reflecting many aspects of City history and of social and economic developments during the last 170 years, is now housed at London Metropolitan Archives.

The image showing constables lined up at Waterloo Station en route to a colleague's funeral is one of only a few early group photographs of officers. The uniforms of the City police are slightly different from those worn by the rest of the British constabulary, with red-and-white chequered sleeve and cap bands (as opposed to black-and-white). Red and white have long been the colours of the City Corporation.

As the City police force was established before motor vehicles appeared on London streets, horses were involved from the beginning, and in 1873 a mounted branch was officially introduced. Horses are particularly useful in the Square Mile; they give officers the ability to see further, travel quickly through small and winding roads, and provide a physical advantage when crowd control is required. The City of London Police is one of the few forces to retain a mounted police section, with stables at Wood Street Police Station, close to Guildhall.

The force has been involved in police work of all kinds since it was set up and now has particular expertise in counter-terrorism, along with tackling fraud and other economic crimes. They have also had their share of high-profile cases. In December 1910 a small gang of Latvian revolutionaries attempted to rob a jewellers' shop in Houndsditch by tunnelling through a wall. Their plan was interrupted by the City police, alerted by a local resident, who was suspicious of the noise created by the gang on the Sabbath in the predominantly Jewish East End. The gang was cornered and responded by shooting their way out of the house, killing three unarmed policemen and injuring several others. The Houndsditch murders caused a national scandal, and descriptions of the suspects (such as the one illustrated) were circulated.

This led to 'the siege of Sidney Street', in January 1911, after a tip-off that gang members were hiding at 100 Sidney Street, Stepney. Two hundred officers from the Metropolitan and the City police forces surrounded the house, and a prolonged gun battle ensued, with Winston Churchill (then Home Secretary) in attendance. The house eventually caught fire but nobody surrendered, and two bodies were found when the house was finally entered. **LT**

▲ Constables of the City of London Police
Photographic print, *c.* 1880–1900
LMA CLA/048/CS/01 3.8, B/09/014
box 27/24

DESCRIPTION of Three men and a woman WANTED for being concerned in the murder of three police officers and wounding two police officers by shooting with revolvers to prevent their apprehension for attempting to break and enter a jeweller's shop in this City on the night of 16th instant.

1st - FRITZ - - - - of 59,Grove Street, Commercial Road, E, 24 or 25, 5ft 8 or 9, complexion sallow, hair fair, medium moustache (turned up at ends,lighter colour than hair of head), eyes grey, nose rather small (slightly turned up),chin a little upraised, few small pimples on face, cheekbones prominent, shoulders square but bends slightly forward ; dress, brown tweed suit (thin light stripes), dark melton overcoat (velvet collar,nearly new), usually wears grey Irish tweed cap (red spots), sometimes trilby hat. Locksmith.

2nd. - PETER - - - - ,known as PETER the PAINTER, same address, 28 to 30, 5ft 9 or 10, complexion sallow, hair and medium moustache black, clear skin, eyes dark, medium build, reserved manner ; dress, brown tweed suit (broad dark stripes), black overcoat (velvet collar, rather old), large felt hat, shabby black lace boots.

3rd. - "YOURKA", age 21, height 5ft 8, hair and moustache dark brown, complexion sallow; dress, blue jacket suit, grey cap, had his eyebrows and forehead coloured with rouge. Speaks German fluently.

All Anarchists and believed to be natives of Russia.

4th - WOMAN, 26 to 30, 5ft 4, slim build, fairly full breasts, complexion medium, face somewhat drawn, eyes blue, hair brown ; dress dark blue ¾-jacket and skirt,white blouse, large black hat (trimmed black silk),light coloured shoes.

Please cause enquiry at Lodging-houses and other likely places and communicate any information obtained to this office.

JOHN OTTAWAY
Superintendent.

Detective Department,
City Police Office,
26,Old Jewry,
London, E.C.

▲ Police notice issued for
the capture of armed robbers
Typescript on paper, 1910
LMA CLA/048/CS/01/1.13

▶ Mounted officers of
the City of London Police
Photographic prints,
c. 1880–1900
LMA CLA/048/CS/01 3.8,
B/09/014 box 27/24

The nineteenth-century market

The City houses a number of important historic markets that date back to the Middle Ages as places for the display and sale of produce. Over time they often came to specialise in particular commodities: Billingsgate market, for example, which was originally a general market, began to specialise in fish at least as early as the sixteenth century and is now the UK's largest inland fish market. There are records of Smithfield (which has long been a hub of the meat trade in and around London) as a place for trading livestock as early as the tenth century.

The original Leadenhall market started as an informal marketplace in the fourteenth century, at which people from outside London (known as 'foreigners') were allowed to sell poultry, cheese and butter. The name Leadenhall was taken from the lead-roofed mansion in the shadow of which the traders were allowed to set up their stalls.

Although already being regulated by the City Corporation, in 1411 it came into the possession of Sir Richard (Dick) Whittington, who gave it to the Corporation, under whose auspices it was later extended and reorganised, creating three large courtyards enclosed by buildings. One yard comprised the beef market, at which leather, wool and hides were also sold; another comprised a fruit and vegetable market. But it was as a poultry market, where both live and oven-prepared birds were sold, that Leadenhall was best known. The market really came into its own following the Great Fire in 1666, as it was the only one to survive the flames; after this its special 'foreigner' status was removed, and the market expanded to absorb the displaced City traders.

Although the painting reproduced here suggests that the market was clean, decorous and frequented by a neatly dressed middle-class clientele, in reality it must have been an extremely noisy, smelly and raucous place in comparison to the banks and businesses that surrounded it. Because of this strenuous attempts were made to close it, but when these failed in the face of opposition, the Corporation decided to rebuild it. Designed by Sir Horace Jones (who was also responsible for new markets at Smithfield and Billingsgate) and built in the Victorian Gothic style, the new market opened in 1881. Leadenhall market today retains much of its late nineteenth-century architecture and operates as a pedestrianised shopping precinct.

Andries Scheerboom (1832–1880), the painter of this picture, was born in Amsterdam. He was a member of a circle of romantic painters working there in the middle of the nineteenth century but spent the later part of his life in London, where he settled in 1863. Scheerboom painted landscapes, including beach views with fishermen at work, as well as townscapes and interiors with lively figures depicted undertaking everyday tasks. JJ

▶ Andries Scheerboom,
Leadenhall Market
Oil on canvas, 1865
GAG 1519

Photography takes off

Small and ephemeral objects help to capture the reality of everyday lives of the past. *Cartes de visite* ('visiting cards') became popular from the 1850s but continued to be produced as family photographs until much later. They typically measure about 2½ by 4 inches.

In Britain, Queen Victoria and Prince Albert were quick to embrace photography to publicise royal family values, and the rest of society followed suit. Here we see an unnamed mother and two children in the photographer's studio, well dressed and portrayed as a genteel, close family, albeit without a father figure present. They do not look into the lens, nor do they smile, which would be seen as showing an immature or foolish character.

Cartes de visite also acted as trade cards for their photographers, who printed their business details on the reverse, in this case Henry Dixon (1820–1893). Dixon trained as a copperplate printer before moving into photography in Watford and then London. He was among the first wave of high-street photographers and moved to Albany Street in 1864. His projects included work for the City Corporation, photographing the building of the Holborn Viaduct in 1866–69 and later working for the City Sewers Commission. These works formed part of wide-ranging improvements to London's health and transport infrastructure that swept away large areas of older streets and buildings. London Metropolitan Archives holds many of Dixon's prints from these projects, forming an important pictorial record of Victorian London. **MM**

◀ Henry Dixon, photographic
carte de visite (front and back)
Photograph and print on card,
c. 1875
LMA SC/GL/TCC/DET-DYS

Entertainment for the masses

The City Corporation's collections record the history of all kinds of entertainment in London, from the highbrow to the low, including a large collection of theatre playbills and programmes, records for the licensing of entertainment venues, images of theatres and related printed materials.

The 'Greatest Show on Earth' opened at Olympia, London, in November 1889. The vivid cover shown here comes from a sixteen-page programme highlighting the attractions, which included over 1,200 performers, 380 horses, 21 elephants and 32 cages of assorted wild animals. Visitors to the show included the British royal family and the writer Rudyard Kipling.

Phineas Taylor Barnum (1810–1891, shown on the left of the cover) was born in Connecticut, USA, and began his career as a showman in the 1830s. He managed Chang and Eng, the original Siamese twins, and General Tom Thumb, the famous dwarf performer. Showmanship was a hard business; fortunes were made and lost, with frequent takeovers of attractions and enterprises. Exploitation of people and animals with unusual physical characteristics was rife, and they received little care once their popularity had waned.

In 1871 Barnum moved into circus management and in 1881 entered into partnership with another great nineteenth-century showman, James A. Bailey (1847–1906, shown on the right). Born James McGinnis in Detroit, Bailey had toured the world, building up his show-business experience. After Barnum's death Bailey carried on for a further fifteen years. 'The Greatest Show on Earth' still exists today, as Ringling Bros. and Barnum & Bailey's Circus. **MM**

▶ Programme advertising
P. T. Barnum's Circus
Printed in 1889
LMA SC/GL/Circuses – Barnum

The Huntley archives

London has long been a centre for migration of people from across the world, and it is important that the City's collections represent the diversity of its population. In recent years a number of important Black and Caribbean community archives have been acquired, building on projects of the early 2000s that explored this area, such as Moving Here, an online image database concerning migration to Britain, and Black and Asian Londoners, which focused on the Black and Asian presence in parish registers from the sixteenth century.

The Huntley archives were deposited by Eric Huntley (b. 1929) and his wife, Jessica (b. 1927), Black political activists and publishers who played a prominent role in the Black Caribbean community. They emigrated from British Guiana (later Guyana) to London between 1957 and 1958. They met Dr Walter Rodney (1942–1980), a Guyanese academic historian and political activist who studied at the School of Oriental and African Studies during the 1960s. In 1968 the Jamaican government banned Rodney for his radical Marxist philosophy, and for teaching students and Rastafarians about the intellectual, sociological and military prowess of ancient African civilisations. The resulting 'Rodney Riots' triggered the development of Black Power, pan-Africanism and political awareness on a global scale.

In reaction to the ban, the Huntleys helped to mobilise support and arranged the printing and street distribution of Rodney's lectures. This culminated in their founding Bogle-L'Ouverture Publications Ltd in 1969, named in honour of Paul Bogle and Toussaint L'Ouverture, both figureheads of Black rebellion against the Caribbean slave trade. The firm became a political weapon to spread Rodney's works further afield. The first publication was the collection of his lectures *The Groundings with My Brothers*. This was followed in 1972 by *How Europe Underdeveloped Africa*, a seminal work by Rodney on the history of post-colonial liberation struggles. Following Rodney's murder in Guyana in 1980, the Huntleys kept his legacy alive by renaming their bookshop the Walter Rodney Bookshop and organising public memorials and anniversary lectures in his name.

The archive comprises 50 linear metres of records, from 1952 to the present. These include authors' files with original manuscripts and correspondence, publications, photographs and films, documenting grassroots publishing across the African Caribbean Diaspora. Papers also document the Huntleys' political, educational, community and family activities in London and internationally. Correspondence, case files, posters and leaflets survive for over twenty organisations in which the Huntleys were active participants. These include campaigning groups such as the Black Parents Movement and the Committee Against Repression in Guyana. The former was established to safeguard Black community rights in British society and sought to challenge the treatment of Black youth by the police, particularly after controversial events such as the 1979 Southall riots. The Committee Against Repression in Guyana was founded in reaction to the news that senior members of Guyana's leading opposition party, the Working People's Alliance, including Walter Rodney, had been arrested after an explosion that destroyed Guyanese government offices in 1979.

The motivating force behind the Huntleys' preservation of their records has been their belief in the power of the written word and in the importance of history in education. This faith in the power of archives to promote community involvement and learning has led to the establishment of annual Huntley Archive conferences, held mostly at London Metropolitan Archives, which focus on the history of Black Caribbean publishing, the impact of Rodney and his work, the Black supplementary school movement, and campaigning. The conferences have showcased the relevance of archives to current issues concerning the community and have attracted new audiences, with the engagement of young people as a significant objective. Youth groups that have been involved have included the Black Experience Archive Trust, the Writing, Acting and Publishing Project for Youngsters and the Manchester Supplementary School. Further deposits of Black Caribbean material have included the archives of Clapton Youth Centre (a Black youth centre in Hackney), Hansib Publications Ltd (publishers specialising in newspapers and books covering African, Afro-Caribbean, Indo-Caribbean and Asian community issues and subjects) and the papers of Sybil Phoenix, the first Black woman to be awarded an MBE. **MR, RW**

◀ Walter Rodney, *The Groundings with my Brothers*
Printed in London, 1969, front cover
LMA 4462/E/01/029

▶ Published greetings cards, Bogle-L'Ouverture Publications Ltd
Printed in London, 1970s
LMA 4462/E/02/006

◀ Selection of soft toys left at the Russell Square/Tavistock Square memorial gardens
LMA 4469/B/03/014

▼ Poem left at the Russell Square/Tavistock Square memorial gardens
Typescript on paper, 2005
LMA 4469/B/03/005

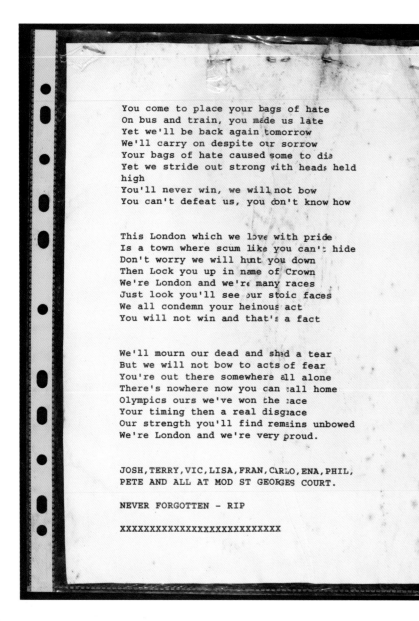

You come to place your bags of hate
On bus and train, you made us late
Yet we'll be back again tomorrow
We'll carry on despite our sorrow
Your bags of hate caused some to die
Yet we stride out strong with heads held high
You'll never win, we will not bow
You can't defeat us, you don't know how

This London which we love with pride
Is a town where scum like you can't hide
Don't worry we will hunt you down
Then Lock you up in name of Crown
We're London and we're many races
Just look you'll see our stoic faces
We all condemn your heinous act
You will not win and that's a fact

We'll mourn our dead and shed a tear
But we will not bow to acts of fear
You're out there somewhere all alone
There's nowhere now you can call home
Olympics ours we've won the race
Your timing then a real disgrace
Our strength you'll find remains unbowed
We're London and we're very proud.

JOSH,TERRY,VIC,LISA,FRAN,CARLO,ENA,PHIL,
PETE AND ALL AT MOD ST GEORGES COURT.

NEVER FORGOTTEN - RIP

XXXXXXXXXXXXXXXXXXXXXXXXXXX

7/7

On 7 July 2005 London was brought to a standstill by four co-ordinated suicide attacks on its transport systems during the morning rush hour. The first three bombs exploded at 8.50 a.m., within seconds of each other within the London Underground network: the first on an eastbound Circle Line train between Liverpool Street and Aldgate; the second on a westbound Circle Line train that had just left Edgware Road; the third on a southbound Piccadilly Line train travelling between King's Cross and Russell Square. The final bomb detonated almost an hour later, on an eastbound number 30 bus, in Upper Woburn Place, close to the British Medical Association building. The bus had been diverted through Upper Woburn Place as a result of the earlier explosion on the Piccadilly Line and was carrying extra passengers who had been forced to find alternative means of transport owing to the earlier attacks. In total fifty-two people, including the four bombers, were killed, and hundreds more wounded.

The attacks prompted feelings of horror and sympathy all over the world, and memorial gardens were established close to the scenes of the attacks to provide a focal point for public mourning. In the days and weeks following 7 July hundreds of mementoes were left at the memorial gardens by families, individuals, businesses and organisations from around the world, in a variety of languages. Some were personal testaments to those killed, injured or missing; others were more general reactions to the events or expressions of religious belief. In addition, hundreds of books of condolence were compiled, again from all parts of the globe, and forwarded to the Greater London Authority.

The books of condolence and all the items from the memorial gardens were collected by London's local authorities and presented as a gift to London Metropolitan Archives between August and November 2005. The artefacts collected from the memorial gardens and tribute sites include greetings cards and cards from floral tributes, poems, postcards, posters, scarves and banners, soft toys, flags and garlands. **NiA**

8/7/05
Me and my wife use us
this Station every day!
It could have been one
of us in your place.
So you shall never
be forgotten, and
God will help to
bring those murderers
to justice.
Love Ron & Sharon

I've never been prouder
Of being a Londoner than
I am now. London has
shown such strength, dignity
and resolve at this most
horrifying of times. It
won't break London, it
will become part of its
unique DNA. London
will become extraordinary
now, its all it can do.
George

This tradgedy and your suffering
will remain embedded in our minds.
   The sacrifice you have made at
the hands of these people will only
serve to strengthen our resolve —
They will not crush our spirit.
   god bless

To Do
ACTION
No
July 2005
ARGENTINA
iS WITH YOU
LONDON

▲ Selection of inscribed cards left
at Edgware Road Underground station
LMA 4469/B/02/006

CHAPTER FOUR

Growth and Renewal

The City has been shaped partly by people and the things they have done, but also by its buildings, street layouts and urban development. The City is very much a place with a distinctive presence, whose look and feel are different from those of other parts of London. Although it may seem at first glance to be dominated by modern glass towers and post-war corporate buildings, it also retains a wealth of earlier buildings along with a layout and street names that recall its medieval origins. The conjunction of old churches and livery halls with imaginative contemporary architecture is part of its special flavour. This chapter focuses on ways in which the collections reflect the City's spatial evolution, which has been driven both by natural incremental growth and by the need for large-scale renewal after major disasters.

The City Corporation's map collection is one of the most significant in London, with particular strengths around the cartography of the capital itself. The standard bibliography, *Printed Maps of London* (1964), states that 'the three most important collections of printed maps in London are those in the British Museum [now in the British Library], the Guildhall Library and the London County Council Library'. As these last two have now been brought together in a unified City collection held at London Metropolitan Archives, the usability as well as the cohesiveness of the overall collection have been enhanced. Choosing particular items from this huge wealth of material is difficult, and the few maps included here are just a tiny sample from this major resource.

The Great Fire of 1666 is regularly, and rightly, recognised as a landmark event in the City's architectural development, as the wholesale destruction of large parts of the streetscape created both the need and the opportunity for extensive new-build. The collections include a range of documentation around the fire and its aftermath, including paintings and maps as well as the very rich archive of plans relating to Wren's reconstruction of St Paul's. Nearly 400 years later,

the Blitz during the Second World War was another time when large swathes of the City were damaged or destroyed, and once again the collections include both graphic and documentary testimony to the effects of the bombs and the rebuilding that took place afterwards. We should, however, remember that fire has been a regular scourge of the City throughout its history; the first known fire of London took place in AD 125, when about a fifth of the Roman city is thought to have been destroyed, and St Paul's Cathedral in its Saxon guise was burnt down in 1087. The notebook of a contemporary tradesman, Nehemiah Wallington, gives eloquent testimony to the fire that overtook London Bridge in 1633, while the nineteenth-century conflagration of the Royal Exchange is graphically captured in the ingenious 'protean view' devised by a Victorian publisher.

The Barbican Centre is another phoenix that rose from the ashes of destruction, and the archives include extensive documentation of the planning and opening of this remarkable feat of post-war urban design. Residentially, architecturally and culturally the Barbican is integral to the City landscape and is one of the Corporation's many gifts to London. Now recognised as a site of special architectural interest, its concrete towers and walkways enclose the ancient church of St Giles Cripplegate and sections of the medieval London Wall.

Getting around this streetscape is another theme of this chapter, with illustrations of the development of transport in the nineteenth and twentieth centuries. Bridges have been an essential part of London's infrastructure for as long as it has been a settlement, and although we know very little about the structures of Roman and Saxon times, we are sure that there was something in place. The records of London Bridge stretch back almost to the very beginning of its construction in stone in the late twelfth century (see p. 101), and from that point onwards the archives include all kinds of documentation, drawings and plans relating to the several bridges that came under the City Corporation's aegis and which are now maintained through the City Bridge Trust.

London Bridge

London Bridge has a long history, spanning almost two thousand years, but there are few written records before the twelfth century. We believe that some kind of timber bridge was built by the Romans and reconstructed during Saxon and early Norman times. Such references as we have are mostly found in chronicles and sagas; they are tantalisingly brief and relate almost without exception to disasters, fire, flood, storm and military assault. The transformational decision to build a stone bridge, towards the end of the twelfth century, is attributed by monastic chroniclers to a London clergyman, Peter, chaplain of Colechurch, who began work on the scheme in or around 1176. The new bridge of nineteen arches resting on twenty piers was a major undertaking. It was built slightly upstream of its timber predecessor, took thirty-three years to construct and was not completed until 1209, four years after Peter's death.

This indenture of grant of property is sealed with the first known seal of London Bridge, made of green wax in the pointed oval shape known as a vesica. It records a grant by Peter de Colechurch, described as 'proctor of London Bridge',

of a house and land in the parish of St Dionis Backchurch to Gilbert de Waltham, carpenter, at an annual rent of 10 shillings. Its exact date is unknown, but it must have been made when work was well under way, but before completion (as Peter was still alive). The City parish of St Dionis is centred on Lime Street and Fenchurch Street, but its church is no longer extant as it was demolished in the nineteenth century.

Houses were built on the bridge, trade flourished and a growing income stream developed from rents and bequests made for the bridge's upkeep. Tolls were levied on carts going over it and ships passing under it, so a dedicated fund was established associated with the bridge, administered from Bridge House, at its southern end. It was this fund that allowed the City Corporation to construct Tower Bridge (opened in 1894) and also to acquire Blackfriars and Southwark bridges. The City Bridge Trust, a charity administered by the City, is now responsible not only for the maintenance of these bridges, and the new Millennium Bridge by St Paul's, but also for distributing surplus funds for a range of charitable causes to benefit the inhabitants of Greater London. **ES**

CIVITAS LONDINVM

Charterhous

Fynesburie Feyld

S. Giles

Bogge hous

More Feyld

More Gate

All Holoues in y Wall

Bustroppes Gate

Buclersbury

The Banck

The bolle bayting

The Beare bayting

London

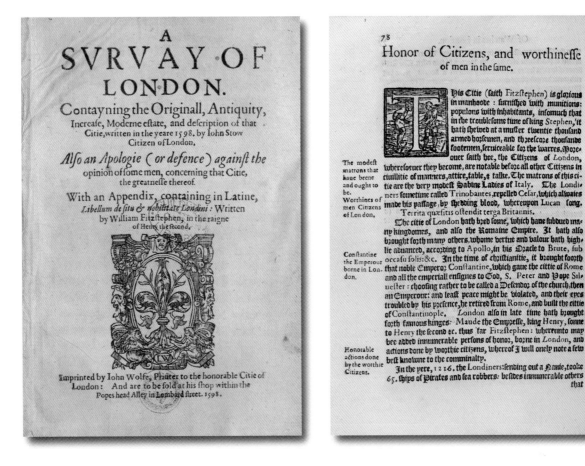

Mapping the City

Selecting maps from the very extensive holdings in the City collections is difficult, as there are many rare and interesting examples from which to choose. This is one of the earliest printed maps of London, known to exist in only three copies (the others being in the National Archives and at the Pepys Library in Cambridge). It shows the layout of Tudor London some time between 1561 and 1570; the exact date is uncertain and has to be surmised from the presence or absence of particular landmarks.

The map was printed on eight sheets, which do not fit together particularly well; the edges of the woodblocks appear to have been damaged at some stage. The map is drawn from a bird's-eye perspective of the landscape, to a scale of roughly 28 inches to the mile. The central section, covering Southwark Bankside to Finsbury, with Cheapside at the centre and London Bridge at lower right, is shown here. All three surviving early copies were printed some time during the reign of James I (who came to the throne in 1603), as his arms were added to the original woodblocks (not shown in this sheet).

This is usually referred to as the 'Agas map', because it was attributed in the eighteenth century to the Elizabethan surveyor Ralph Agas (1545–1621). This is certainly erroneous, as Agas would have been too young to produce it, and it does not reflect his usual style. **DAB**

John Stow's *Survay*

John Stow was born in the parish of St Michael, Cornhill, in 1525. Although the son of a tallow chandler, he did not follow his father's trade but was apprenticed to a merchant tailor, eventually establishing his own business in the parish of St Andrew Undershaft. By the 1560s Stow's interests in history and antiquarianism had led to the publication of his *Summarie of Englyshe Chronicles*, which was frequently reprinted. After many years of further research Stow produced what was to become his most famous work, *A Survay of London* (1598), which has been in print, almost without a break, for over four hundred years.

Stow's prose style is simple, anecdotal and amusing, but it is his minute account of the buildings, social conditions and customs of the City of London that we value so much today. He recorded a city that within just two generations would be swept away by the Great Fire of 1666. In an age only just beginning to develop topographical illustration and detailed mapping, Stow's written description of churches, tombs, livery halls, conduits, streets and markets is often the only information historians have on the topography and history of many London buildings and streets. His anecdotes and memories also provide information that would have otherwise been lost.

Guildhall Library holds many editions of Stow, but the most treasured is this first edition of 1598. It retains much of its original simple vellum binding and has an inscription showing that its first owner purchased it on 21 June 1599 for 2 shillings. **PR**

Fire in the City

Fire has always been an urban hazard, a bringer of disaster and then an opportunity for renewal. The fire that comes most readily to mind in the context of London's history is the Great Fire of 1666, but there has been no end of smaller conflagrations over the centuries. An early, Saxon version of St Paul's Cathedral was destroyed by fire in 1087, while more than a hundred houses in Cornhill were burnt in 1748. A preponderance of wooden structures, built close together, always made for high fire risk.

An earlier seventeenth-century fire, which destroyed many houses on London Bridge in 1633, was chronicled by Nehemiah Wallington (1598–1658), a Puritan turner who lived in the parish of St Leonard Eastcheap with his wife, Grace, and their five children, four of whom died in infancy. His notebook relates how the fire began in the house of John

Briggs at the City end of the bridge. It burnt fiercely, and Wallington conveys with journalistic detail the panic as people fled. The Thames was at low tide, and despite the best efforts of the brewers from Southwark, who brought water, the fire continued to burn into the following week. Wallington visited the scene and described holding 'a live cole of fire in my hand'. He also listed the forty-three houses destroyed and the trades of their inhabitants.

Wallington believed the fire to be a judgment on London's sins, and he also catalogued at length the sins of contemporary London, the 'idolatry, superstitcion … adulteries, fornication, murthers, oppressions' that he saw around him. His notebook is valuable not only for its historical details but also for its insights into the thoughts and concerns of an ordinary Londoner of the period.

1633   *479*

A Thankfull Remembrance

Come and behold the workes of God. he is terrible in his doings
toward the Sonnes of men psalm LXVI
It is the Lord that formeth the Light and createth the darknes: he maketh
peace and createth evill. I the Lord do all these things   Isaiah XLV 7
There is no euill in the Cittie which the Lord hath not done it Amos III 6
It is the bounden dutie of vs all that haue beene the beholers of the
wonderfull workes of the Lord our God his mercyes and iudgments shewed
heretofore. and now of Late of a fearefull fire: wee should not forgett itt our
selues. and we should declare it to all others. euen to ye generations to Come
Take heed to thy Selfe. and keepe thy Soule diligently: that thou forget not ye
things which thy eyes haue seene. and ye they depart not out of thine heart all
the days of thy Life. but teach them thy Sonnes. and thy Sonnes. Sonnes
Tell you your Children of it. and Let your children shew it to their children
and their children to another generation
For the workes of the Lord are greate: and ought to be sought out of all them
that Loue him psal CXI 2
O God thou hast taught me from my youth: euen vntill now: therefore wh
will I tell of all thy wondrous workes psalm LXXI 17

One the XI day of February (being monday 1633) began by Gods iust hand
a fearefull fire in the house of one M John Brigges neere ten of the Clocke
att night, it burnt down his house and the next house with all the goods that wer
in them and as I heere that Briggs his wife and childe Maid escaped with their liue
verie hardly hauing nothing on their bodies but their shirt and smoke: and
the fire burnt so fearcely, that itt could not be quenched till it had burnt
downe all the houses on both sides of the way from S Magnes Chruch to the
first open place. And although there was water enough very neere: yet
they could not safely come at it, but all the Conduittes neere were opened
and the pipes that caried watter through the streets were Cut open. and ye
watter swept down with broomes with helpe enough. but it was the will of
God it should not preuaile And the hand of God was the more seene in this
in as much as no meanes would prosper. For the 3 Engines which are
are such excellent things, that nothing that euer was deuised Could do so
                                                                          much

The fire of 1633 was as nothing compared with the destruction wrought by the Great Fire in September 1666, when the medieval City was almost entirely destroyed over three days. It started in a baker's shop in Pudding Lane, to the north of London Bridge. Within hours it was beyond control, and by the time it was finally checked it had destroyed an estimated 13,000 houses, 87 of the 109 parish churches, 43 livery halls and the Royal Exchange, as well as St Paul's Cathedral. Although there were few recorded deaths, nearly nine-tenths of the City's then population of 80,000 saw their homes destroyed.

The view of the fire in this painting was probably taken from near the Inner Temple Gardens, with Old St Paul's silhouetted against the fiery red sky. The outline of the composition resembles an etching by Wenceslas Hollar, which may have been used as a source. The painting is attributed to a contemporary artist known only by his surname, Waggoner, on the basis of another painting by him formerly belonging to the Company of Painter–Stainers, which was destroyed in the Second World War.

Many maps were produced showing the extent of the fire. Doornick's (overleaf) provides a clear depiction of the magnitude of the disaster. An inset panoramic view with hand-coloured flames licking against the night sky infuses the necessary drama into the scene. At the top left we see one of the proposals for the rebuilding of London, favouring a very rational grid-like plan. This trilingual map, published in Amsterdam, also highlights the level of international interest in London's disaster. **NA, JS, ClT**

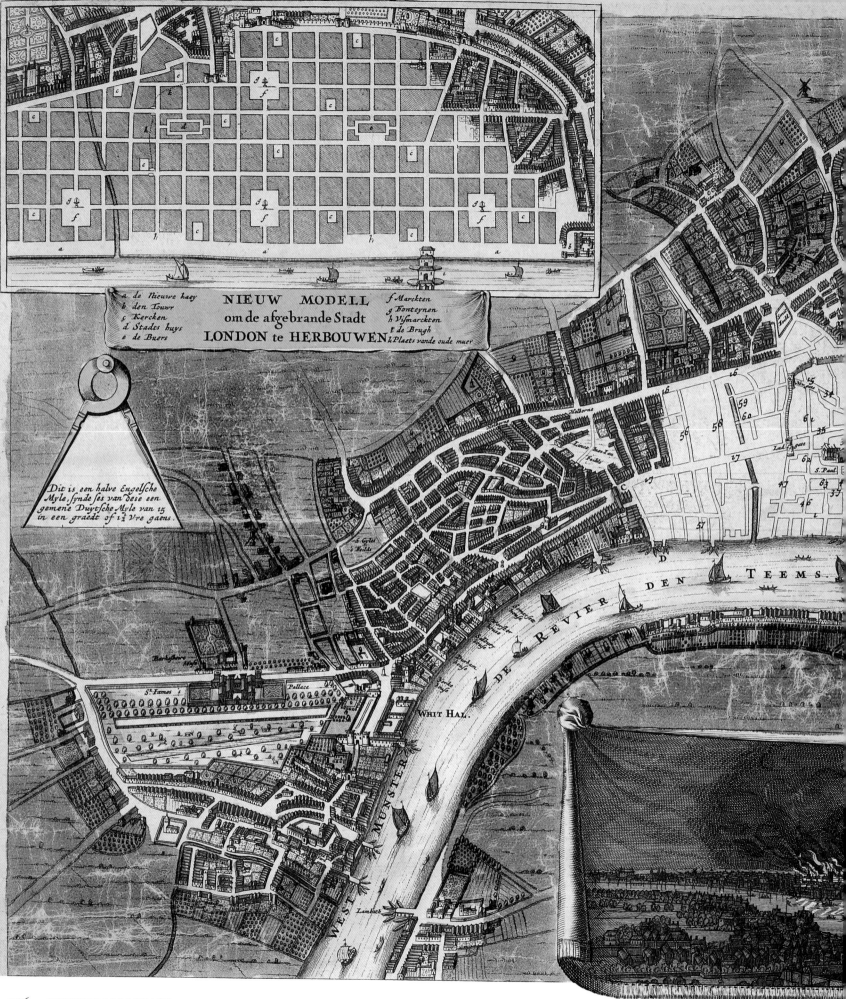

NIEUW MODELL
om de afgebrande Stadt
LONDON te HERBOUWEN

a de Nieuwe kaey
b den Touvr
c Kercken
d Stadts huys
e de Buers
f Marckten
g Fonteynen
h Vismarckten
i de Brugh
k Plaets vande oude muer

Dit is een halve Engelsche
Myle, synde ses van dese een
gemene Duytsche Myle van 15
in een graedt of 1¼ Vre gaens.

DE REVIER DEN TEEMS

WHIT HAL.

WEST MUNSTER

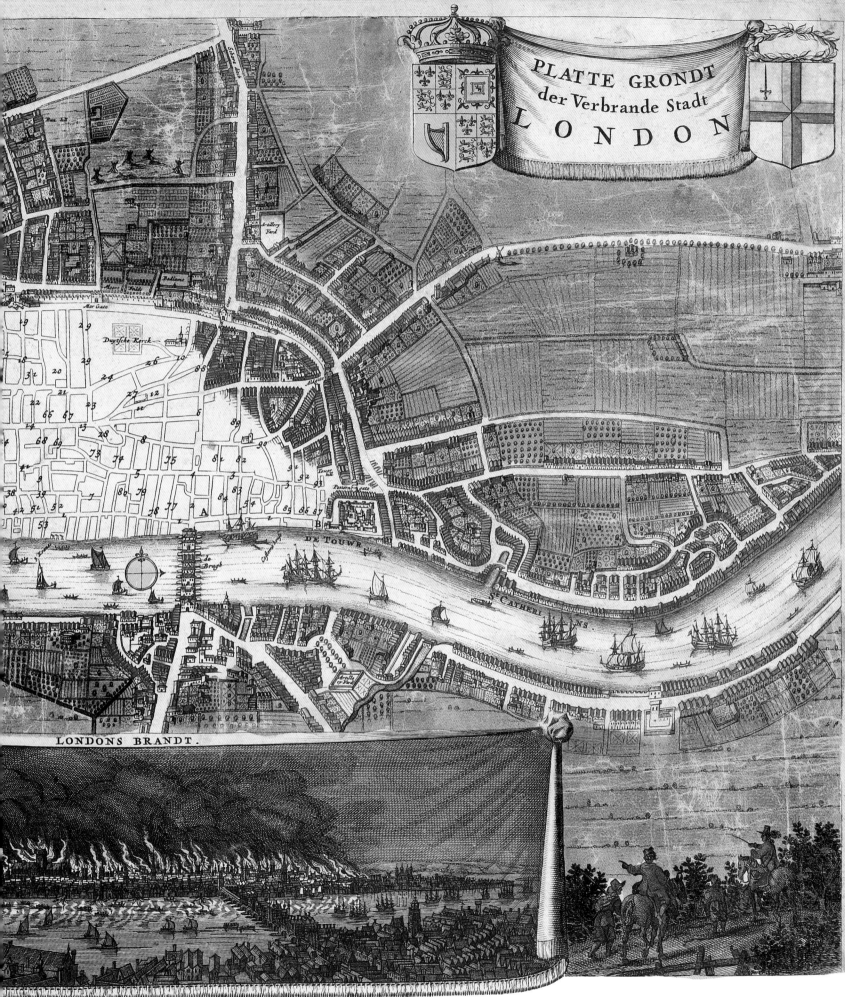

PLATTE GRONDT
der Verbrande Stadt
LONDON

LONDONS BRANDT.

◀ Thomas Wyck, *St Paul's Cathedral in Ruins after the Great Fire*
Ink and wash drawing on paper, *c.* 1667
LMA SC/GL/SLD/001

Rebuilding St Paul's

Many of the images that we have of London's catastrophe in 1666, such as Waggoner's painting, show the entire City dramatically covered with smoke and flames. Ease of recognition and speed of execution were key attributes for publishers and their engravers, so that exciting snapshots were available for use in broadsheets and for transmission far beyond London. In some cases a generous quantity of billowing smoke was simply added to a pre-existing view of the city skyline. More potent, but less common, are views from positions in the midst of the fire-damaged streets. Thomas Wyck's small sketch of St Paul's Cathedral in the aftermath of the disaster shows skeletal Romanesque arches open to the elements and the exposed crypts surrounded by dust and rubble.

Suggestions for the rebuilding of London after the fire were quick to appear. One of the City surveyors, Richard Newcourt, came up with a proposal to create a geometrically planned grid-pattern city, consisting of fifty-five perfectly regular precincts, each centred around a church. Similar schemes were suggested by John Evelyn, Robert Hooke and Christopher Wren. In the event, theoretical considerations for the building of an 'ideal' City were quickly overtaken by practicalities and commercial pressures; nobody could afford to buy out all the landowners so as to be able to remodel the landscape completely.

Among the more high-visibility decisions to be taken in the aftermath of the fire were those relating to the rebuilding of

St Paul's Cathedral, whose architectural future had already been under discussion earlier in the seventeenth century. Sir Christopher Wren, who had been advising on repair work for the cathedral before the fire and who was the architect of numerous post-fire City churches, was officially commissioned to design the new building in 1668. The process was a long one, with numerous fresh starts and designs rejected along the way, and even during the late 1670s, while the foundations and walls were being built, many of the most fundamental decisions about the form and final appearance of the building had yet to be taken.

One advantage of this evolutionary design process was that windfalls such as the threefold increase in coal tax dues assigned to the cathedral from 1685 could be factored into the creative process. Wren, with his assistant Nicholas Hawksmoor, was able to recast his design along more ambitious lines. This sketch, from the extensive set of drawings and building accounts deposited with the City Corporation, represents a key moment in the evolution of the final design for the dome, making it taller and more assertive than first envisaged. Ideas continued to develop throughout the following decade, and the dome and lantern as eventually built were even grander than imagined here. The cathedral was finally completed in 1710. **JS**

▶ Nicholas Hawksmoor,
design for the dome of
St Paul's Cathedral
Pencil, pen and ink on paper,
c. 1690
LMA St Paul's Cathedral Deposit
(Downes 95)

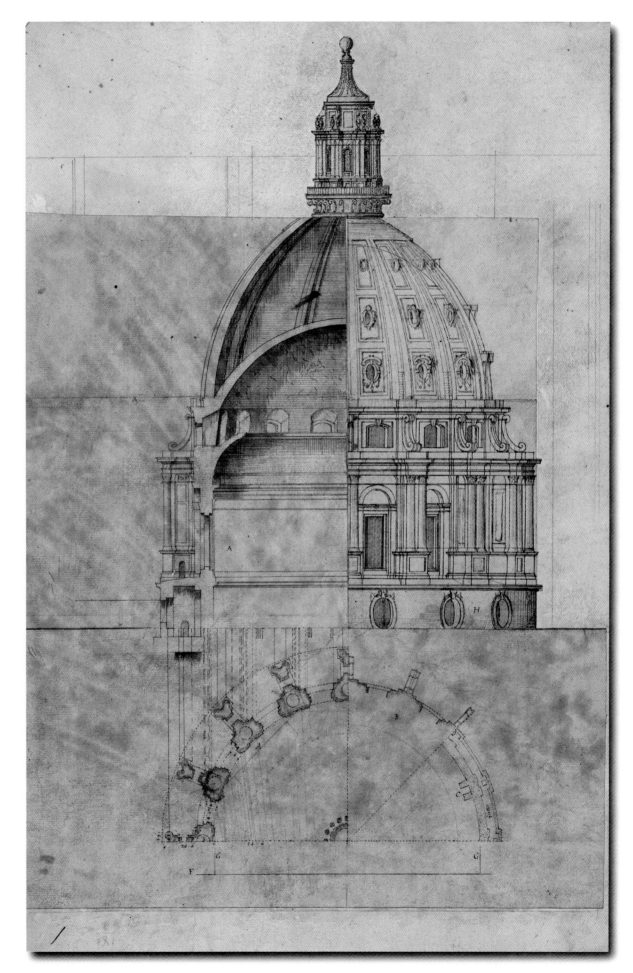

◀ Unknown artist, *Prospect
of the City from the North*
Oil on canvas, *c.* 1730
GAG 4449

▲ Nicholas Hawksmoor,
letter to the Chelsea
Waterworks Company
Manuscript on paper, 1734
LMA ACC/2558/MW/C/15/347/1

Water supplies

London could be said to owe its very existence to its good
supply of fresh water. It was one of the major factors that led
the Romans to settle there in the first century AD. Water was
typically drawn from wells and springs, as well as from the
Thames and its tributaries; these sources remained adequate
until the thirteenth century, when the increase in population
meant that it became necessary to seek additional means of
supply. In 1581 the City Corporation granted a lease to Pieter
Morice, a Dutchman, to create the first mechanical supply
water in London, using an ingenious waterwheel at London
Bridge to pump water to Cornhill.

(continues on next page)

(continued from previous page)

Water was also brought from outside the City, using conduits to convey it from further and further afield. At the beginning of the seventeenth century the need for more drastic measures was evident, and the Corporation obtained Acts of Parliament allowing it to bring water from springs in Chadwell and Amwell in Hertfordshire. In 1609 these powers were transferred to Sir Hugh Myddelton and his newly formed New River Company.

The company opened the New River in 1613 with a waterway that brought supplies to its headquarters in Clerkenwell, from where they were conveyed through pipes to domestic and business customers. The painting *Prospect of the City from the North* was completed just over a century later and shows the New River Head complex in the foreground, with the famous Round Pond to the centre left. The pond remained in operation until 1914, and to the present day the Clerkenwell area retains architectural evidence of this aspect of its historic past (which is reflected in many of its street names).

The New River Company remained the largest of the increasing number of commercial suppliers of water to London until the late nineteenth century but was challenged in the west of the capital particularly by the Chelsea Waterworks Company. The company had been established in 1723 'for the better supplying the City and Liberties of Westminster and parts adjacent' and took its supply from the Thames, storing it in low canals around the present site of Victoria Station. It also set up reservoirs in Green Park and in Walnut Tree Walk in Hyde Park and was successful initially because of its ability to provide water for the royal palaces and government offices. The letter of 1734 from the architect Nicholas Hawksmoor, who was at that time Secretary to the Board of Works, indicates the care that the company had to take in dealing with such influential customers and the detail they needed to manage so as not to 'lessen or impair the Beauty and Ornament' of Hyde Park. **GP**

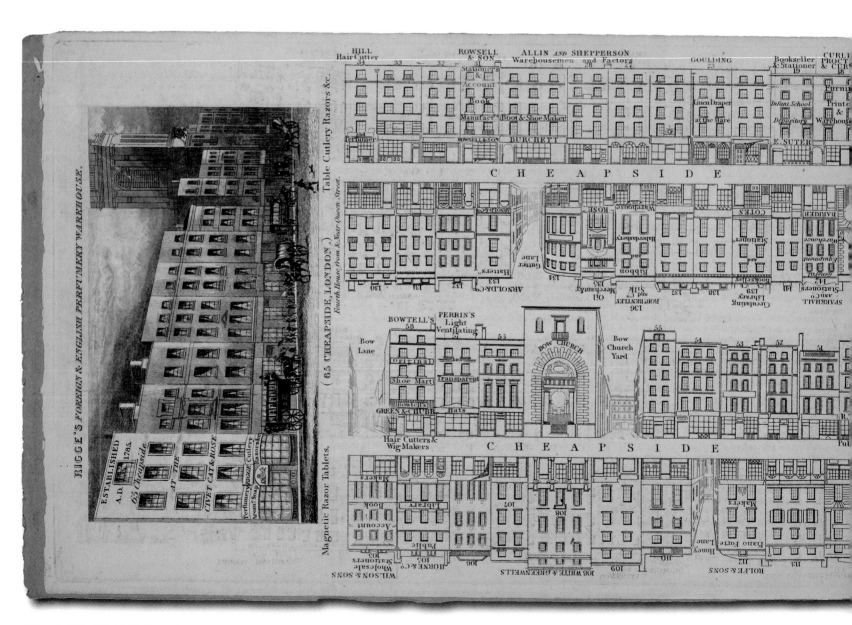

The early Victorian City

'One of the wonders of the present age … a most singular and successful effort to depict a plan of London, by giving a representation of each street, with the front of every house.' So wrote a contemporary reviewer of *Tallis's London Street Views*, a serial publication issued between 1838 and 1840. It was the brainchild of John Tallis, an enterprising young London bookseller whose later career included establishing an American agency, creating a rival to the *Illustrated London News* (after trying to buy it) and recovering from bankruptcy. Each part depicted the elevations of both sides of a major London street, engraved with a map of the surrounding area and a view of the street itself or a shop or famous building there. The issues cost just 1½ d. apiece; much of the cost of production was covered by the sale of the advertising space on the cover and spare pages.

Tallis's Street Views is unique in attempting to show every shop and building front on each chosen street. It provides a snapshot of the London landscape of the time, representing the Georgian City of low-rise individual houses and shops. These would soon afterwards be transformed by Victorian entrepreneurs, whose viaducts and bridges, new roads and railways gradually obliterated many of the buildings depicted here. Sets of *Street Views* are extremely rare. The one held by Guildhall Library is believed to be the only complete copy in existence as it retains not only the full text but also the original wrappers, which were usually disposed of when the parts were bound up.

The view shown here, of part of Cheapside, has been altered almost entirely, by our Victorian ancestors, by the Luftwaffe in the Blitz and by post-war town planners. Just one point remains fixed and identifiable, at the corner of Wood Street, where a row of two-storey shops at 123–26 Cheapside is almost unchanged. Perhaps most remarkable of all, the plane tree behind the shops in St Peter's churchyard is still there today, bigger, broader and resilient. **PR**

▼ John Tallis, *Tallis's London Street Views*
Printed in London, 1838–40, part 42
GHL SR

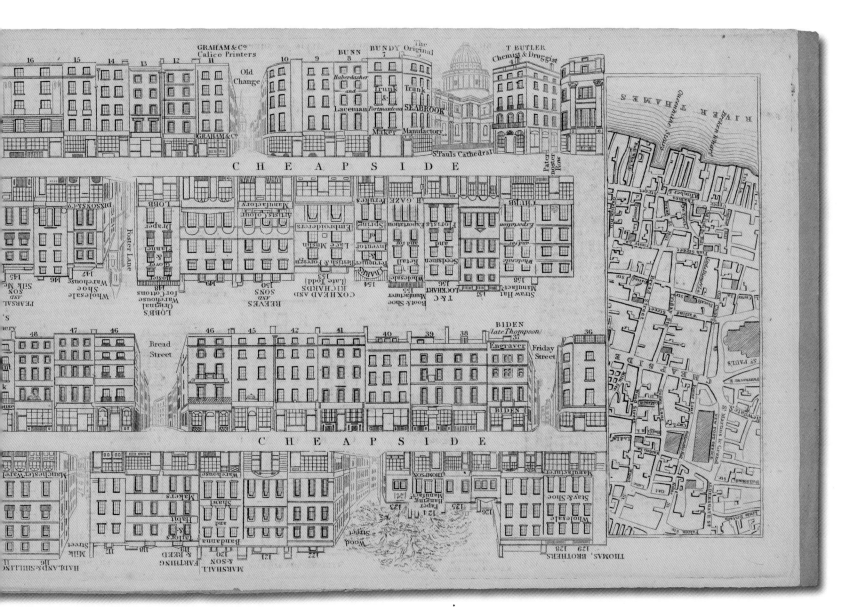

Fire again

As the Victorian era began, the Royal Exchange was by far the most important commercial building in London. It was engulfed by flames and burnt to the ground on a single night in January 1838, the worst such disaster in the City since the Great Fire. Several important institutions had their offices in the Exchange; it was in one of them, the coffee house of Lloyd's (see p. 56), that the fire is thought to have begun. Fighting the fire was hampered by the extremely cold temperature, which rendered many of the fire engines useless when the water supplies froze. The fire spread quickly, and it became a question more of protecting neighbouring sites than of saving the Exchange.

The flames could be seen as far away as Windsor Castle, and the scene was depicted by many artists. The prints that were published included this ingenious 'protean view', which shows the Exchange both before and after the onset of fire. It used a second transparent layer behind the top sheet, which when brightly back-lit (preferably with a dedicated viewing device) transformed the scene. Several early nineteenth-century publishers, and particularly William Spooner and William Morgan, experimented with transparent views like this. Fires were something of a gift to them, as they otherwise had to content themselves with night and day transformations, festive illuminations and the occasional volcanic eruption.

The fire engines attending the Royal Exchange fire in 1838 were all marked with the names and arms of the insurance companies they represented, there being no public service fire brigade at this time. Firefighters were particularly overwhelmed in 1861, when a massive blaze consumed several major warehouses, and the goods they contained, at Tooley Street, fronting the Thames close to London Bridge. The massive losses suffered by the insurers were tragically compounded by the death, in fighting the blaze, of the much respected Captain of Brigades James Braidwood. The need for a public force was acutely felt, and the Metropolitan Fire Brigade was formed shortly afterwards. It was controlled initially by the Metropolitan Board of Works, whose extensive archives (part of the wider London Government Collections) include a wealth of material illustrating the history and techniques of firefighting in the capital.

This sober promotional poster celebrates the immaculate discipline of the Metropolitan Fire Brigade's ladder-scaling drill, but it is primarily a piece of Victorian advertising by the firefighting equipment manufacturers, Shand Mason & Co. During the 1860s and '70s they produced various stirring pictures, usually showing their vehicles speeding to a rescue. Their product range was extensive, from steam-powered fire engines to smaller items, hoses and specialist ladders. **JS**

▲ *The Royal Exchange before the Fire, and on Fire*
Lithograph with transparency, 1838
LMA SC/PZ/CT/01/972

▶ *Metropolitan Fire Brigade Scaling Ladder Drill*
Engraving on paper, 1873
LMA SC/GL/PR/LC/LA/045-061

METROPOLITAN FIRE BRIGADE SCALING LADDER DRILL.

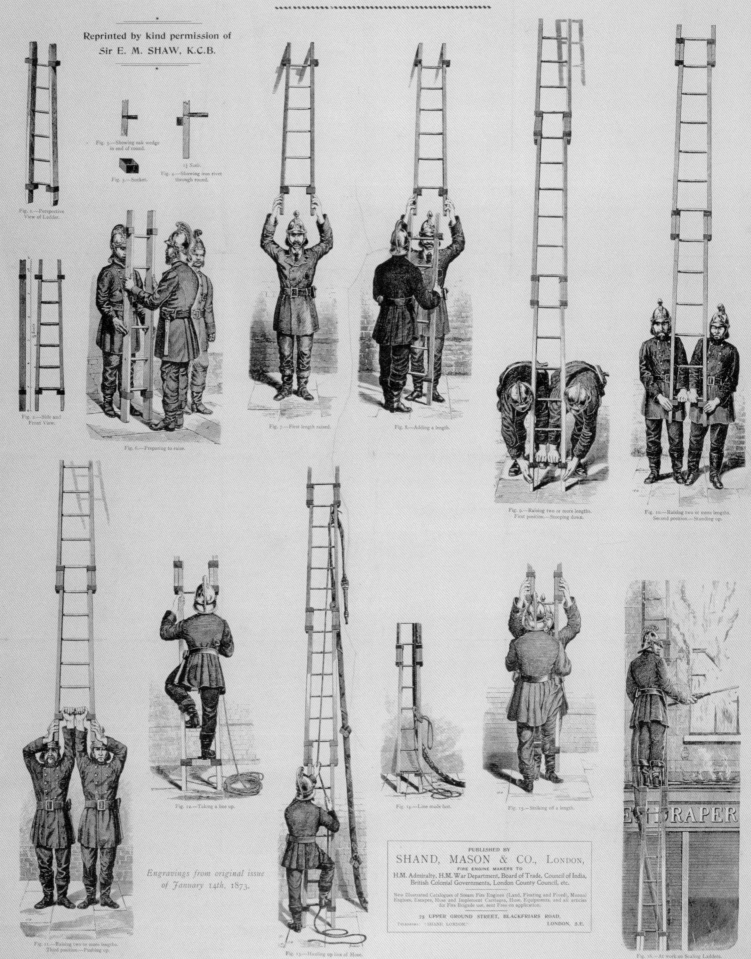

Reprinted by kind permission of
Sir E. M. SHAW, K.C.B.

Engravings from original issue
of January 14th, 1873.

PUBLISHED BY
SHAND, MASON & CO., LONDON,
FIRE ENGINE MAKERS TO
H.M. Admiralty, H.M. War Department, Board of Trade, Council of India,
British Colonial Governments, London County Council, etc.

New Illustrated Catalogues of Steam Fire Engines (Land, Floating and Fixed), Manual
Engines, Escapes, Hose and Implement Carriages, Hose, Equipments, and all articles
for Fire Brigade use, sent Free on application.

75 UPPER GROUND STREET, BLACKFRIARS ROAD,
LONDON, S.E.

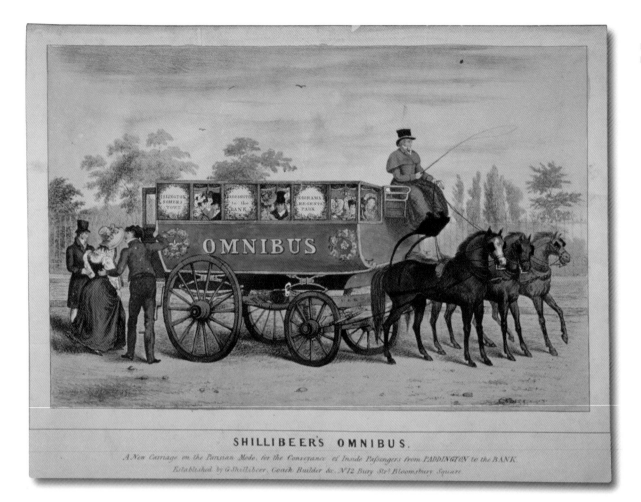

◀ *Shillibeer's Omnibus*
Lithograph, 1829
LMA SC/GL/PR/LC/48/61

SHILLIBEER'S OMNIBUS.

A New Carriage on the Parisian Mode, for the Conveyance of Inside Passengers from PADDINGTON to the BANK.
Established by G.Shillibeer, Coach Builder &c. N°12 Bury Str. Bloomsbury Square.

Nineteenth-century transport

Nineteenth-century London saw a massive expansion both in size and population. Technological and social developments meant that the ways in which people travelled around the City and its suburbs would be radically altered by the end of the century.

In the early 1800s hackney carriages monopolised passenger transport within the City. To travel further afield, short stage coaches travelled to villages surrounding London, which eventually became suburbs. In 1828 a change in the law enabled the creation of the first recognisable omnibus service and a challenge to the dominance of the hackney carriage.

George Shillibeer was a London coach-builder who was inspired by a new mode of transport emerging in Paris. The omnibus, introduced in 1819 by a Parisian banker named Lafitte, carried a dozen or more passengers over set routes through the French capital with cheap pre-set fares. The idea was ripe for exploitation in London, and Shillibeer began his omnibus service with two carriages in the summer of 1829. The route started in Paddington and ran along the New Road (now Marylebone Road, Euston Road, Pentonville Road and City Road), skirting the northern fringes of London, and went through the City to terminate at Bank. The service ran daily, at set times and with fixed prices, and commenced regardless of how full the carriage was, a novelty in itself.

The image here shows one of Shillibeer's smart, liveried conductors assisting a lady up on to the bus. Up to twenty passengers could sit inside, protected from the weather, a contrast with other coaches, where less comfortable space was available on the roof for a lower fare. Only ten years before this, the chill that the poet John Keats caught, which began the decline of his health, was attributed to his travelling on the exposed roof of a coach from the City to Hampstead.

The omnibus concept proved very popular, and competitors began running similar services on various new routes. Shillibeer was unable to compete and was declared bankrupt in 1831. His omnibus continued, though, and in time the disparate companies operating the services were regulated and brought together to form the basis of the London bus system we know today.

The arrival of rail transport in London began in 1836 with the opening of the London and Greenwich Railway, terminating at London Bridge station. Mainline termini connecting London with other cities to the north opened up along the New Road, with Paddington, Euston and King's Cross all in operation by the 1850s. There was then no easy way of transporting increasing passenger numbers from these termini to the City; the resulting congestion was a problem, to which the solution was the construction of a new underground railway running through the northern railway stations to Smithfield. This beginning of the London Underground system is documented in a series of photographs held at London Metropolitan Archives.

▶ *At Baker Street Looking East (London Metropolitan Railway)*
Photographic print, July 1862
LMA SC/GL/HFL

▼ *Dignitaries Seated in an Open Railway Wagon at Edgware Road Station (London Metropolitan Railway)*
Photographic print, July 1862
LMA SC/GL/HFL

This was the first time an underground passenger railway system had ever been built, and it called for a new method of construction in order to try to reduce costs and disruption. The 'cut and cover' system involved cutting a trench beneath existing roads and building a brick tunnel over the tracks before covering it over and reinstating the road surface. The image at the top here shows workers posing on top of the scaffolding over the 'cut and cover' construction at the junction of Marylebone Road and Baker Street.

Construction took three years, and chief engineer, John Fowler, resplendent in his white top hat, took his seat alongside other notable dignitaries (including the future Prime Minister, William Gladstone) on a trial run along the route in May 1862. The party is pictured here at Edgware Road station in open-topped carriages provided by the building contractors; passengers had covered carriages once the route opened.

The Metropolitan Railway began operating in January 1863 and was an immediate success, with over 27,000 journeys a day during the first year. Five years later another underground railway, the Metropolitan District Line, opened between Westminster and South Kensington. Eventually the lines connecting the railway termini were joined to form the Inner Circle Line and railway companies began extending their lines outwards in order to exploit the potential of reaching the London suburbs. The beginnings of the Underground system we have today were well in place. **KS**

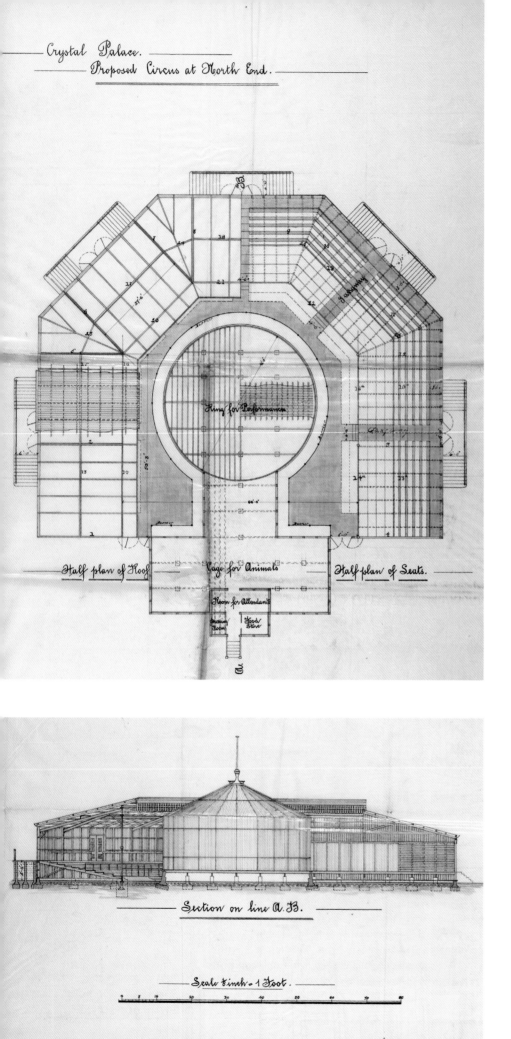

Crystal Palace.
Proposed Circus at North End.

Half plan of Roof *Cage for Animals* *Half plan of Seats.*

Ring for Performance

Room for Attendant

Section on line a. B.

Scale ⅜inch = 1 Foot.

◄ Plan and elevation of
proposed extension at the north
end of Crystal Palace (details)
Pen and ink, watercolour on
paper, 1891
LMA GLC/AR/BR22/002586

The beauty of plans

The London Government Collections include over 17,000 files from the late nineteenth to the late twentieth centuries created by the Architects' Department of the London County Council and Greater London Council, under the requirements of the London Building Acts. These called on architects, builders and property owners to submit plans of buildings or alterations in order to check that the proposals complied with regulations. Each file generally contains correspondence, a copy of the report to the relevant committee and a set of submitted drawings and plans, often in colour. A single case file can include a number of applications relating to the same building over a long period of time and provide graphic evidence of how it changed in use or appearance over the years. These files are a goldmine of information on the development of London buildings over the period and are much valued by contemporary planners and surveyors as well as by architectural historians.

The collection includes plans of theatres, cinemas, clubs, restaurants and cafés, schools, houses and flats, hotels, churches, mosques and synagogues, railway and Underground stations, and many of the most notable public buildings, such as the Royal Opera House, Harrods, Selfridges, the Ritz and the Royal Albert Hall. There are also designs for more unusual buildings, such as air-raid shelters, beauty salons, chocolate factories, cycle tracks, dairies, pram sheds, a monkey house, fish and chip shops, a 'switchback railway' and even a grotto. Shown here, as one example from the many that could be chosen, is a drawing for an extension to the Crystal Palace dating from 1891.

A separate but also valuable collection of plans and drawings is found in the archive of the Hampstead Garden Suburb Trust. The development of Hampstead was the brainchild of Henrietta Barnett, the wife of Canon Barnett, co-founder of the Whitechapel Art Gallery and Toynbee Hall. Rooted in the ideas of Ebenezer Howard and the Garden Cities Movement, the concept of a planned housing development grew out of the campaign to prevent the open space and farmland to the north-west of Hampstead Heath from being swallowed up by speculative builders. The archive includes over 6,100 plans and licence applications forming an almost complete architectural record of this unique and famous exercise in town planning. Included are signed and hand-coloured linen plans by Raymond Unwin and Barry Parker, Edwin Lutyens and many others.

Henrietta Barnett believed it was possible to enhance the living conditions of the working class by providing a harmonious combination of buildings and nature. Further, by planning a wide diversity of housing types, she hoped that the resulting mixed community would break down class barriers. The new suburb's low-density housing (eight houses

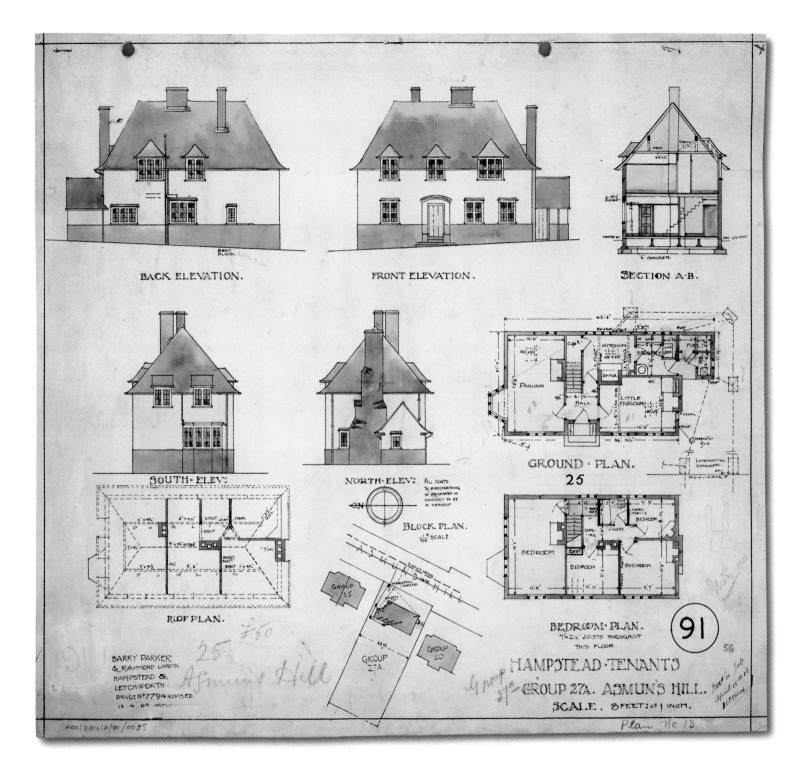

BACK ELEVATION.

FRONT ELEVATION.

SECTION A·B.

SOUTH·ELEV:

NORTH·ELEV:

BLOCK·PLAN.

GROUND·PLAN.
25

ROOF PLAN.

BARRY PARKER
& RAYMOND UNWIN
HAMPSTEAD &
LETCHWORTH·
DRWG: N° 7794 REVISED·

BEDROOM·PLAN.

HAMPSTEAD·TENANTS
GROUP 27A. ASMUN'S HILL.
SCALE. 8 FEET: 1 INCH.

▲ Plan of 25 Asmuns Hill
Pen and ink, watercolour on paper, 1908
LMA ACC/3816/P/01/035

to an acre) was intended to harmonise with the landscape around it and to offer accommodation for both rich and poor. It was hoped that the result would avoid the worst evils of conventional suburbs of the time: uniformity, social segregation and the destruction of the countryside.

The suburb was developed over the period 1907–30 and has altered very little since then, owing to the enforcement of strict planning regulations. In 1986 the London Borough of Barnet designated it a Conservation Area, and on 28 November 1996 over 500 of the earliest buildings, with their original Arts and Crafts doors, tiles and fireplaces, were added to the English Heritage register of listed buildings as Grade II, while nearly thirty of the larger houses were upgraded from Grade II to Grade II*. **DB**

Charting the Blitz

The archive collections include a great wealth of material chronicling life and conditions in London during the Second World War. There are civil defence records from both the London County Council and Middlesex County Council, who also dealt with the evacuation of children from the London area. Records of the London Ambulance Service and the London Fire Brigade include air-raid fire reports. Photographs and art works from the period together with official circulars, policy papers, posters and flyers help to illustrate life in wartime London.

This photograph shown here is part of a collection of 370 images taken between 1940 and 1944 by two City of London Police Constables, Arthur Cross and Fred Tibbs, who were tasked with recording bomb damage in the Square Mile (their image of the Barbican site is shown on p. 125). In this particularly dramatic shot the façade of 23 Queen Victoria Street collapses as firemen try to save it. The night of 10–11 May 1941 saw the last but heaviest raid of the London Blitz, which had begun the previous September. Huge fires were started in the London docks, Westminster Abbey and the Palace of Westminster were badly damaged, and Poplar Hospital had to be evacuated. Almost three thousand people were killed and injured across London.

The map illustrated opposite is part of a set compiled by the London County Council War Damage Survey Section, showing the accumulated effects of bomb damage in London during the course of the Second World War. The section shown covers the western half of the Square Mile. The maps are based on the 1:2,500 scale Ordnance Survey maps of 1916, updated by the LCC around 1940, showing London as it was on the eve of the Blitz; 110 sheets were made, covering 117 square miles, including the City of London and the twenty-eight metropolitan boroughs then in existence. Similar maps were compiled for other British cities, but the LCC set developed the most comprehensive colour-coding system for recording damage to buildings and property. Black indicates an area of 'Total Destruction', while purple represents 'Damaged Beyond Repair' (which, in the map here, includes most of the buildings around St Paul's Cathedral, and huge swathes of the City east and north of there). Progressively lighter colours indicate lesser degrees of damage. The position of V1 flying bombs and V2 rockets, which landed in 1944–45, is also represented by circular symbols (several can be seen on this example).

As well as the damage to London's homes and buildings, the bombing during and after the Blitz of 1940–41, coupled with later V1 and V2 attacks, resulted in over 85,000 Londoners being killed and injured. The bomb damage maps offer a comprehensive visual record of the extent of wartime damage to the fabric of inner London and highlight the huge problems that post-war planning and rebuilding programmes had to cope with. **MM**

▲ Tony Castle, poster advertising
London Tramways
1926
LMA LCC/TWYS/02/030

▶ Harold Workman,
Chaos on London Bridge
Oil on canvas, *c.* 1938
GAG 4174

Growing pressures on transport

Trams were a common sight in London throughout the first half of the twentieth century, before being phased out during the early 1950s. A collection of colourful posters held at London Metropolitan Archives reminds us of their former importance as part of London's transport infrastructure.

Until the early nineteenth century London's people and goods were transported by river or by hackneys (four-wheeled coaches for hire). Developments during the nineteenth and twentieth centuries saw a network of modes of transport grow up around the capital (see p. 116). At the beginning of the twentieth century electric tramway systems began to appear in Greater London, of which the London County Council Tramways (LCCT) was the most extensive.

By the early 1920s the LCCT was in competition with the Underground Group, who ran most of London's buses and underground railways as well as several tramway companies. LCCT decided to commission a set of posters from the London County Council's Central School of Arts and Crafts, one of the country's leading art schools. The original set was designed in black and white, although following their success further posters were commissioned in colour. Further commissions from other sources followed.

Some posters advertised journeys to specific places, promoting London as a tourist attraction. Others focused on London as a shopping destination, such as the Christmas poster shown here, aimed at encouraging shoppers into London to take advantage of an all-day ticket.

Traffic congestion in London is nothing new, and Harold Workman's slightly tongue-in-cheek depiction of mid-twentieth-century chaos on London Bridge is probably only slightly inaccurate. The site of London Bridge has been the City's most important crossing point for almost two thousand years, ever since the Romans established a river crossing (probably a simple timber structure) near by. It was not until the late twelfth century that a more permanent stone structure was constructed (see p. 101), which, although taking over thirty years to complete, stood for over six hundred years.

Old London Bridge was itself finally demolished in 1832, having made way for a new bridge designed by John Rennie. Constructed in stone between 1824 and 1831, the bridge incorporated a series of five semi-elliptical arches, with the building work itself being supervised by Rennie's son, also named John. This 1831 bridge was widened in 1902 but still proved to be inadequate for the needs of a modern city, unable to cope with the ever-increasing demands of vehicle and pedestrian traffic – well illustrated in Workman's painting. In 1965 the decision to rebuild was again made, and a new concrete and box girder construction, faced with polished granite, was built quite literally around its predecessor. This new London Bridge was opened by the Queen in 1975.

Harold Workman (1897–1975) was a painter in oil and watercolour who specialised in landscapes, architectural and interior subjects. He studied at Oldham and Manchester, and his paintings will be found in numerous permanent collections across England. He also taught art and was at various times a lecturer at the Architectural Association, the Sir John Cass College and the Hammersmith School of Arts and Crafts. **JJ, ST**

▲ *Corporation of London Newspaper*
March 1968
LMA COL/AD/07/01/006

The Barbican

The Barbican is one of the landmarks of the modern City landscape, a case study in post-war urban planning and a striking expression of the modernist aesthetic of its time. Its maze of reinforced concrete towers and elevated walkways, with an international arts centre surrounded by residential apartments, prompts a range of reactions, but it cannot be ignored. As Pevsner's *Buildings of England* has it, 'there is nothing quite like the Barbican Estate in all British architecture.' The City Corporation's archives include extensive documentation on its planning, construction and opening.

The site has a long history. It was the northern gate of a Roman fort, built around AD 120, and then a city gate in London Wall which was completely rebuilt in early medieval times. The gate was finally demolished in 1760 so that the street could be widened. The surrounding area, known as Cripplegate, often had an undesirable reputation for overcrowding and disease, but as the home of Grub Street it was also a centre for poets and writers. Celebrated residents of the Tudor period included Thomas More, Ben Jonson and Sir Martin Frobisher.

It was the total destruction of the area during the Second World War that made the creation of the estate possible. The image of a bomb-levelled St Giles is one of a large series of images taken by two City of London Police officers (Arthur Cross and Fred Tibbs) who were told to go out at first light after bombing raids and photograph the damage. The photograph shown here is just one example from this unique and moving collection, many of which show locals surveying the ruins.

Plans for redevelopment began in 1952, when there were only fifty-eight people living in the entire ward. It was a bold experiment in urban living, and it was a brave decision by the Court of Common Council to support it and see it through. The architects Chamberlin, Powell and Bon submitted many plans and revisions between 1954 and 1968. Work finally began in 1965 and was not completed until 1981. Many would say that the name – the Barbican – is appropriate for the rather fortress-like character of the buildings, but its extensive network of walkways and open spaces includes gardens and water features. It was designed around the idea of a complete residential experience, with shops and a built-in car park as well as theatres and cinemas.

The flats – just over two thousand in all – were deliberately built to be compact and were handed over to their first tenants undecorated, to allow them to personalise the space to reflect their own tastes. It has been a desirable address ever since it opened, and apartments are always in high demand. The arts centre was planned originally to be for residents only, but its potential was soon realised, and today it has become the largest multi-arts centre in Europe and the home of the London Symphony Orchestra. A public library at the heart of the centre was an integral part of the vision. The complex became Grade II listed in 2001 and has been designated a site of special interest for its scale, cohesion and architectural ambition. **LT**

▲ Arthur Cross and Fred
Tibbs, *The Barbican Estate Site
after Bombing*
Photographic print, 1941
LMA SC/GL/PHO/A/258/6/1

▶ Prospectus for the
Barbican estate
c. 1980
LMA SC/GL/NOB/A/045/10

The GLC and modern London

This poster from the archives of the Greater London Council (GLC) not only exemplifies a major civic project in modern London but also hints at the huge wealth of other material on the development of the twentieth-century metropolis to be found in the London Government Collections at London Metropolitan Archives. The Thames Barrier, sponsored by the GLC, was begun in 1974 and was officially opened by Queen Elizabeth II in 1984. It stretches 520 metres, from Silvertown on the north bank of the Thames to Charlton on the south, and protects 125 square kilometres of central London from the danger of flooding from tidal surges. The barrier's central gates, each 20 metres high and made of steel weighing 3,500 tonnes, can be closed within fifteen minutes. The poster is taken from a set of records relating to the barrier that also includes committee files on the decision-making and design process and many photographs of the site at all stages of construction.

This is just one of countless projects that have shaped today's capital whose development can be traced through the archives. The governing bodies of modern London have created landmarks such as the Royal Festival Hall, County Hall and the Thames Embankment, but they have also been responsible for housing estates, schools, fire stations, roads, hospitals and sewers, and many other things that affect how people live in London.

The collections not only include documentation of all these but also reflect the evolution of the various bodies that have been created to administer London since the nineteenth century. The expansion of the capital from the early decades of that century onwards put increasing strain on the inherited system of local government, which divided responsibility between the City Corporation and the surrounding counties. The City resisted pressure to extend its geographical coverage, and a Metropolitan Board of Works was established in 1855. This was succeeded by the London County Council in 1889, which was succeeded in turn by the Greater London Council in 1965. The GLC was abolished in 1986, when its powers were devolved to the London boroughs; in 2000 a pan-London body was recreated in the form of the Greater London Assembly, with an elected mayor. Each of these created, or interrelated with, a host of other organisations, such as the Inner London Education Authority, the London Passenger Transport Board and the Metropolitan Asylums Board. The ways in which Parliament sought a definitive solution for the government (or control) of London is an important strand of political and constitutional history that runs through these many changes and reshapings.

The scale of the capital meant that the services created by the various authorities were often large-scale, innovative and potentially controversial. The Metropolitan Asylums Board provided London's first (horse-drawn) ambulance service and started the use of radium for cancer treatment in 1928. In the 1930s Herbert Morrison, leader of the LCC, was instrumental in creating what became the Green Belt to control urban development. The Right to Buy scheme pioneered by the GLC for its housing stock in the 1970s was adopted by the Thatcher government on a national scale a decade later. The GLC's policies on equality were much disparaged in the 1980s but were the forerunners of ideas that became more widely accepted not long thereafter. The congestion charge introduced by the Mayor of London in 2003 has become a blueprint for use by cities elsewhere around the world.

The London Government Collections in which all this activity is documented, which are still growing, run to over 73,000 archive boxes, 48,000 bound volumes, 300,000 photographs and 8,000 folders of plans. **DB, CS**

◀ Greater London Council,
poster for the Thames Barrier
c. 1984
LMA GLC/DG/PRB/08/03514

The modern printmaking tradition

Although the City Corporation's graphic collections are most commonly celebrated for their great historic strengths, they continue to be selectively augmented with appropriate contemporary material that chronicles London. This fine print is one of the most recent new arrivals to join the collection of prints, drawings and photographs curated at London Metropolitan Archives.

Anne Desmet's engraving is one of an extended series of prints entitled 'Olympic Metamorphoses' that the artist worked on during 2009–10, showing many different aspects of the London Olympics site under construction. It not only brings into the collections an example of the work of a celebrated contemporary London printmaker but also captures an artistic response to this major project in the life of the metropolis. In 2012 London becomes the first city in the world to have officially hosted the Olympic Games three times, having also been the venue in 1908 and 1948. The Olympic Park in Stratford, a few miles east of the City, is a 500-acre site whose stadiums, buildings and landscape will be adapted after the Games to new permanent recreational and residential uses.

Anne Desmet was born in Liverpool in 1964 and studied at the Ruskin School of Drawing in Oxford and the Central School of Art and Design in London. She currently lives in Hackney, not far from the Olympic site. Her specialisms include wood-engraving, linocutting and mixed media collage, and she has explored streetscapes and architectural themes in London and Italy, where she had a British School at Rome scholarship in 1989. Her work will be found in many permanent collections around the world and has won numerous international awards; the example shown here won the 'best print in any category' accolade at the Royal Academy Summer Exhibition in 2010.

The bird's-eye viewpoint was a deliberate choice to try to evoke the scale of the construction project and the visual interest of the emerging shapes. That artistic concept, and the use of relief printmaking, in which the lines are commonly cut from a wooden block, connects this picture with one of the earliest depictions of London held in the collection, and one of the first complete visual records of the city that exists, the Tudor map view known as the 'Agas map' (see p. 102). JS

The Arts and Sciences

The City Corporation's collections include a range of material that has particular literary, artistic or scientific value, quite apart from whatever historic City association may underpin its presence or acquisition. Sometimes this is accidental, in the sense that archives may include references to the famous as well as to the less so; poets are baptised, or hauled before the courts, in the same way that tailors or butchers are, and are just as likely to appear in the records. Oscar Wilde's prison record is entered in the register alongside that of others who are now wholly forgotten and who are not likely to stimulate the same degree of interest. Official documents with blank spaces among their leaves may be used to jot down literary musings that come to be more highly regarded than the accounts that comprise their substantive purpose.

The Corporation's art collection, whose contents are drawn on to make the changing display that is always on show in Guildhall Art Gallery, has featured in earlier chapters but appears here more in its own artistic right. It too has its roots as much in documentation as in art for art's sake, as the beginnings of the collection lie in the Fire Judge portraits commissioned in 1670 in acknowledgment of the important work undertaken by those judges after the Great Fire. The emphasis on portraiture and civic occasions broadened out once the idea of a dedicated gallery space was adopted towards the end of the nineteenth century, after which the blossoming of the collection took place with the acquisition of major Pre-Raphaelite and other Victorian works. Some of the iconic highlights from the collection are reproduced here, along with examples from the discrete and particularly important group of Dutch and Flemish paintings given by Lord Samuel in 1987. Another significant twentieth-century gift was the studio collection of Sir Matthew Smith.

Although graphic art is most visibly represented in the City Corporation in the gallery, there is also an enormous wealth of prints and drawings curated alongside the maps at London Metropolitan Archives, and the examples from the Willshire Collection included here constitute only a tiny taster of the material available to explore. The photographic holdings associated with the London Government Collections run to at least 300,000 images from across London taken during the late nineteenth and twentieth centuries.

Although John Keats spent his last London days in Hampstead and died in Rome, he was very much a City man by birth and up-bringing, and spent his early years just north of Guildhall, where his father ran the Swan and Hoop Inn, close to what is now Moorgate station. It was therefore appropriate for the Corporation to take over the running of Keats House in Hampstead, close to the Heath, one of the City's open spaces. This brought with it not only the fabric of what is now a very successful museum but also some important documentary and artefactual material associated with Keats, some of which is shown here. The letter from the dying Keats to his fiancée, acquired in 2011 with the aid of the Heritage Lottery Fund and others, was a wonderful addition to these items and a testament to the City's commitment to the ongoing development of the collections.

When small displays of the most iconic City documentary treasures are wanted for high-ranking diplomatic visits, the manuscript that is most likely to accompany Magna Carta and the 'William Charter' is the Shakespeare deed, which tends to eclipse even a particularly perfect copy of the first folio. Irrational though it may be, there is a long history of attaching value through association: people have long been moved by being in the presence of things that have been touched by saints or heroes. The deed has genuine historical value in recording a property transaction undertaken by the great man in his later years, but the fact that this is one of so few surviving documents to which we know he put his pen is what tends to inspire awe. Whatever the motives that move people to value historic collections – which are many and varied – let us not try to judge between them but celebrate the fact that they do.

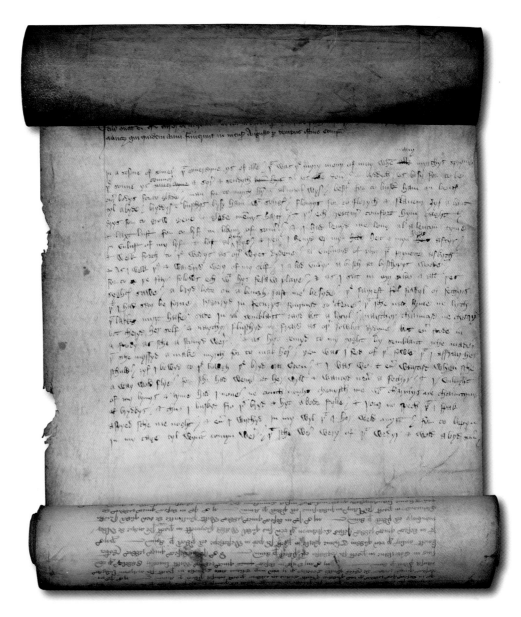

Medieval poetry

Historical documents may contain things that are incidental to the main content but which become part of their value – indeed, they may come to be of more interest to later generations than the core content. Bookbindings may be constructed using fragments of other, earlier books, margins may be annotated or drawn in, and the blank spaces in account rolls may be used for writing literary rather than financial material.

On a spring day in 1396 or 1397 John Tickhill, chantry clerk and collector of the rents of St Paul's Cathedral, went walking out from the cathedral eastwards through the City, towards Bishopswood in Stepney, beyond the City walls. He was seeking there to sit 'in his solas' after a gloomy 'Lentyn tyme'. Although not university-educated, Tickhill was a cultured man, interested in science, astronomy and poetry: he had read Langland's *Piers Plowman*. Some time later he wrote out his alliterative verses on to the back of one of his old cathedral account rolls, by that time no longer a current record. The results, beginning 'In a sesone of somere that soverayne ys of

alle', are no literary masterpiece but show how poetry as a genre was familiar to men like him. Tickhill remained a churchman and soon afterwards moved to become rector of St Gregory by St Paul, a parish church against the south side of the cathedral. He died around 1423. The verses that he composed were not discovered until 1980, when the archives of St Paul's Cathedral were deposited with the City Corporation.

It was perhaps passing through Aldgate, over which, until recently, Geoffrey Chaucer had had his lodgings and where he had composed *Troilus and Criseyde*, that inspired Tickhill to put his mournful encounter with a bird in the woods into verse. Chaucer (c.1340–1400), generally acknowledged as the greatest poet of medieval England, was very much a City man. The son of a Thames Street vintner, he spent most of his life in London and may have been educated at St Paul's Cathedral's almonry school. In 1378 he was appointed comptroller in the port of London, and the City's letter books record the grant to him by the mayor of London of a lease for life, rent-free, of a property over Aldgate. **MP**

Prints from the Willshire Collection

The Willshire Collection is an important collection of early graphic prints, including woodcuts, engravings and etchings, assembled by a medical doctor, William Hughes Willshire, and bequeathed to Guildhall Library in 1899. Willshire conceived his collection in broad terms to provide a comprehensive overview of the history of printmaking. The collection includes etchings by Rembrandt, woodcuts and engravings by Dürer and the work of many other celebrated artists; most of the major schools and techniques in European printmaking are represented.

The small and simple woodcut shown here, hand-coloured with gold and silver leaf added, was made in southern Germany. The maker is not known, and it is one of only two impressions of the print known to survive today. It illustrates the story of St Veronica, who was believed to have offered Christ a handkerchief on the road to Calvary, which miraculously received an imprint of his face. Small prints like this were favoured as charms or amulets, especially by pilgrims; the hand-written inscription round the frame translates as 'Hail the face of the Lord, I pray to you, have mercy upon me. Amen.'

Wenceslas Hollar's famous views of seventeenth-century London are well represented in the collections (see p. 53); the print of velvety muffs shown below would have been admired by Willshire for the technical brilliance with the etching needle required to achieve such fine detail. The Rembrandt etching opposite is one of his many prints showing people reading, or interrupted from reading. Rembrandt liked exploring the intimacy and concentration represented by a solitary figure studying. **JS**

▲ *St Veronica*
Woodcut on vellum, hand-coloured, *c.* 1475
LMA SC/GL/WIL/001/028

▼ Wenceslas Hollar, *Study of a Muff*
Etching on paper, 1647
LMA SC/GL/WIL/019/025

▲ Rembrandt van Rijn, *Woman Reading*
Etching on paper, 1634
LMA SC/GL/WIL/011/052/A

◀ Cartulary and rental of the estates of the Woodford family
Manuscript on vellum, c. 1510, fols 4v–5r, 9v–10r
LMA CLC/267/MS01756

Sir Thomas More

Thomas More played a hugely important role in English political life in the early sixteenth century. The Lord Chancellor's principled (though some would say wilful) stand in opposing Henry VIII's divorce, and losing his head, have made him something of an iconic figure in popular perception. He had strong links with the City; born just off Cheapside in 1478, he went to school in Threadneedle Street. Then, after service in the household of the Lord Chancellor, Archbishop Morton, and two years at Oxford, he returned to be trained as a lawyer at Lincoln's Inn. He was an under-sheriff for the City in 1510 and probably represented the City in Parliament around that time.

Guildhall Library holds the Cock Collection, a little over 200 rare volumes relating to More collected by Alfred Cock (1849–1898) and bought for the library by public subscription after his death. One of its particular treasures is a copy of the first edition of *Utopia*, More's treatise on the search for an ideal state of government, based on the imaginary island of Utopia, with toleration of religion, universal education and a kind of communism. The collection includes other early editions of *Utopia*, and many of More's other works in early English editions.

More's thinking was much influenced by his contacts with an emerging group of English humanists, such as William Grocyn and John Colet, later Dean of St Paul's, who were actively promoting the revival of classical learning ('Utopia' is derived from Greek οὐ, 'not', and τόπος, 'place'). Through this circle of friends More met Erasmus, the great Dutch humanist, when he first came to England in 1499, and Erasmus in turn introduced More to Pieter Gillis, town clerk of Antwerp, another kindred spirit. It was in Gillis's company that *Utopia* was conceived, while More was staying with him in 1515, and Gillis came to be honoured by being included as a character in the book.

Among his many humanist virtues, More was a poet of great accomplishment and influence. Some of his most important verses in English, the so-called 'Fortune verses', were once thought to survive only in one contemporary manuscript version in Oxford, and from the later printed editions of Robert Wyer (1556?) and More's *Englysh Workes* (1557). Another contemporary manuscript text of the verses was recently discovered among the City Corporation's collections. The lines have been written into a cartulary compiled by Robert Woodford (1460–*c*. 1526) of Burnham in Buckinghamshire for his son Thomas (*c*. 1497–1545). They are arranged in two stanzas per page, with a running heading (possibly suggesting that they were copied from a lost printed exemplar). The stanzas are set opposite nine full-page coloured coats of arms of members of the Woodford family. There is some evidence that the family had links with Thomas More's circle. Internal evidence suggests a completion date for the cartulary around 1518, only a decade or so after the verses themselves are believed to have been written. **MP, JW**

▲ ▶ Counterpart indenture for sale and purchase of a property in Blackfriars
Manuscript on parchment, with detail of signature (right), 10 March 1613
LMA CLC/522/MS03738

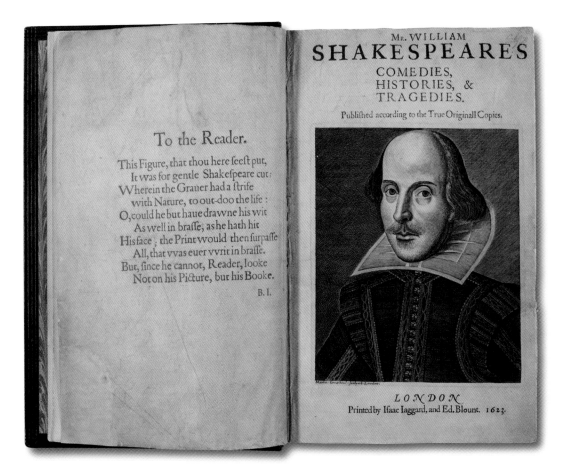

To the Reader.

This Figure, that thou here feeſt put,
It was for gentle Shakeſpeare cut:
Wherein the Grauer had a ſtrife
with Nature, to out-doo the life :
O, could he but haue drawne his wit
As well in braſſe, as he hath hit
His face ; the Print would then ſurpaſſe
All, that vvas euer vvrit in braſſe.
But, ſince he cannot, Reader, looke
Not on his Picture, but his Booke.

B. I.

Mʀ. WILLIAM
SHAKESPEARES
COMEDIES,
HISTORIES, &
TRAGEDIES.
Publiſhed according to the True Originall Copies.

LONDON
Printed by Iſaac Iaggard, and Ed. Blount. 1623.

Shakespeare

The first folio of William Shakespeare's plays, which has been called the most important work in the English language, was published in November 1623. Shakespeare had been dead some eight years by then, and the book was conceived by two of his fellow actors, John Heminges and Henry Condell, as a tribute and memorial. It contains thirty-six of Shakespeare's plays and is of fundamental importance in establishing the Shakespearean canon. It was printed at the corner of Aldersgate Street and Barbican. Between 750 and 1,000 copies are believed to have been printed, which originally sold for between 15s. and £1 each. The engraved portrait of Shakespeare by Martin Droeshout, used as a frontispiece, has become the seminal image of Shakespeare the man, although its accuracy has been much disputed.

About 240 of those original copies survive today, in various states of repair; the Guildhall Library copy is noted in the latest international census of first folios as 'a remarkable copy, both for its completeness and good condition'. Its provenance can be traced back to around 1760, when it was acquired by William Petty Fitzmaurice (1737–1805), 2nd Earl of Shelburne, a great patron of the arts and briefly Prime Minister. At the sale of his library in 1806 it was purchased for the London Institution, from which it was transferred to Guildhall Library in 1912.

Although a first folio is a great treasure, the document on the left is arguably a greater one. There may be several hundred folios surviving, but the City Corporation owns one of only six documents in the world bearing Shakespeare's signature. This is a title deed dating from 1613, when Shakespeare purchased a property in Blackfriars. The vendor is named as Henry Walker, citizen and minstrel of London, while the purchaser was William Shakespeare of Stratford upon Avon, gentleman, supported by three trustees: William Johnson, citizen and vintner of London, and John Jackson and John Hemmyng, both described as gentlemen of London. It is tempting to equate Johnson with the landlord of the Mermaid Tavern, who had that name, and Hemmyng may be the John Heminges who helped sponsor the folio; Jackson's identity is uncertain.

This is the only London property known to have been owned by Shakespeare, but why he purchased it is uncertain. He may have intended to live there, as it was conveniently situated for both the Blackfriars and the Globe theatres, but there is no evidence that he ever did so. It is more likely that he bought it as an investment, or in order to enhance his status as a gentleman.

The property itself, part of which was erected over a great gate, lay in Blackfriars, in the precinct formerly occupied by the Dominican house dissolved in 1538. It abutted on the street leading down to Puddle Wharf, now St Andrew's Hill, and was 'right against the Kinges Maiesties Wardrobe', now commemorated in Wardrobe Place. It had been leased in 1604 to William Ireland, citizen and haberdasher. Shakespeare bequeathed the property to his daughter Susanna Hall, and it came subsequently to her daughter Elizabeth Nash, but it had passed out of family hands by 1667. The deed was purchased by the Corporation in 1843 for £145. **VH**

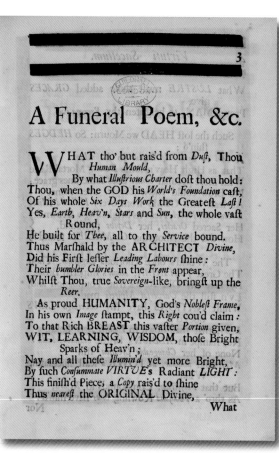

A Funeral Poem, &c.

WHAT tho' but rais'd from *Duſt*, Thou
  Human Mould,
    By what *Illuſtrious Charter* doſt thou hold:
Thou, when the GOD his *World's Foundation* caſt,
Of his whole *Six Days Work* the Greateſt *Laſt!*
Yes, *Earth*, *Heav'n*, *Stars* and *Sun*, the whole vaſt
  Round,
He built for *Thee*, all to thy *Service* bound.
Thus Marſhal'd by the AR CHITECT *Divine*,
Did his Firſt leſſer *Leading Labours* ſhine:
Their *humbler Glories* in the *Front* appear,
Whilſt Thou, true *Sovereign*-like, bringſt up the
  Reer.
  As proud HUMANITY, God's *Nobleſt Frame*,
In his own *Image* ſtampt, this *Right* cou'd claim:
To that Rich BREAST this vaſter *Portion* given,
WIT, LEARNING, WISDOM, thoſe Bright
  Sparks of Heav'n;
Nay and all theſe *Illumin'd* yet more Bright,
By ſuch *Conſummate VIRTUE's* Radiant *LIGHT:*
This finiſh'd Piece, a *Copy* rais'd to ſhine
Thus *neareſt* the ORIGINAL *Divine*,

                                      What

Elkanah Settle, City poet

The outsides of books have long been used as arenas for decoration and display, and the Corporation's collections include many early books, which manifest the craft of bookbinders over the centuries. Noteworthy among these is a group of bookbindings associated with Elkanah Settle (1648–1724), the 'City Poet', who saw an opportunity to use bindings to seek favour.

Settle was an active figure in the literary life of Restoration London, who rose to glory in his twenties by writing plays with considerable success. His play *The Empress of Morocco*, noted by the *Oxford Dictionary of National Biography* for its 'elaborate palace scenes, fleets of ships, imprisoned princesses and violent assassinations' won him favour and a position at court. He had the showman's talent for display and became adept at producing pageants and spectacular theatrical performances; in 1680 he organised a particularly extravagant City pageant costing £1,000. His operatic comedy *The World in the Moon* claimed in the dedication to its published version (1697) to have been the most elaborate dramatic production ever mounted on an English stage. Settle also experienced the ups and downs of fame and found that popular appeal can evaporate as quickly as it can appear. His cause was not helped by his frequent involvement in government affairs, with a knack for supporting the wrong side, and then changing allegiance, several times during the shifting political sands of the 1680s. He was much lampooned by contemporary (and ultimately more famous) writers such as Pope and Dryden, the latter of whom described Settle's work as 'heroically mad'.

In 1691 Settle took over responsibility for organising the annual pageants associated with the Lord Mayor's Show and assumed the title of City Poet. This was an official post vacated by the death of its previous holder, Matthew Taubman; Settle was the last man to be so designated. His literary output turned increasingly to verse, and he sought to boost his income by writing poems to mark weddings or deaths in prominent families. He then sent copies, handsomely bound with the family arms gold-tooled on the cover, to the prospective patron, hoping for financial encouragement by return. If the book was sent back to him unwanted, he might try again elsewhere, as some Settle bindings have a second coat of arms on a new piece of leather pasted over the original. His resourcefulness in recycling did not stop there, as many of his poems have a striking similarity; the first twenty lines of a funeral elegy he wrote and had printed for Earl Cowper in 1723 are identical to the opening lines of this lament for Charles Hedges of 1714. His enterprise met with scant reward, as he died poor, and his burial place is unknown. Towards the end of his life he was reduced to playing the part of a dragon at Bartholomew Fair, dressed in a green leather costume. Guildhall Library has a fine collection of over forty of these Settle bindings, together with good holdings of contemporary editions of his published works. **DP**

The City's art collection

This portrait is one of a series that marks the beginning of the City Corporation's art collection. In October 1666 a commission of six surveyors (three acting for the Crown and three for the City) was appointed to survey the damage of the Great Fire and to put forward proposals for reconstruction. The obligation to rebuild was placed on tenants, and there were often disagreements between them and their landlords over extending their leases to compensate them for their costs. Those who could not rebuild within the specified period also had to be compensated for the loss of their lease when the right to rebuild was sold to someone else who could. While many cases were settled by the wards or the Court of Aldermen, a special commission of royal judges – the Fire Court – was appointed to deal with compensation claims. They sat at Clifford's Inn, and their work was of intense interest to the City Corporation, for rebuilding depended on it.

In 1670 the Court of Aldermen decided to commission portraits of the Fire Judges, in recognition of their important work, to hang in the newly restored Guildhall. It is thought that Sir Peter Lely was the first artist applied to, but that he refused the job because the judges were too busy to come to his studio to be drawn. Four further artists were then considered, and John Michael Wright was given the commission for fourteen portraits in September 1670. Eight more were subsequently ordered, bringing the total to twenty-two by 1675. All were framed in matching but not identical carved and gilded pine frames in the auricular or 'Sunderland' style, which was highly fashionable in the second half of the seventeenth century.

The Fire Judges' portraits were hung in front of the windows in Guildhall, whose lower parts were blocked up, but they soon began to deteriorate and had to be restored. A major restoration in 1779–80 may have involved scouring off Wright's original paint, and by the late nineteenth century it was recognised that little of Wright's handiwork remained to be seen. In 1951 twenty of the series were de-accessioned, as all were in poor condition after the war and the loss of Guildhall Art Gallery during the Blitz left nowhere to hang them. Four now belong to Lincoln's Inn, others survive elsewhere, and only two (*Sir Matthew Hale* and *Sir Hugh Wyndham*) remain in the City's collection.

Wyndham trained as a lawyer at Lincoln's Inn and was called to the Bar in 1629. He was created a Judge of the Common Pleas in 1654 by Oliver Cromwell; removed from office at the time of the Restoration, he became a Member of Parliament for Minehead in 1661, not returning to the Bench until 1670, when appointed Baron of the Exchequer. He again became a Judge of the Common Pleas in 1673 and died at Norwich while on circuit in 1684. **NA, JJ**

▶ John Michael Wright, *Sir Hugh Wyndham, Kt, Judge of the Common Pleas* (detail)
Oil on canvas, 1670
GAG 24

The Samuel Collection

The most significant gift ever conveyed to the City Corporation, the Harold Samuel Collection comprises eighty-four seventeenth-century Dutch and Flemish paintings, offering a vivid glimpse of life and art in the Netherlands' Golden Age.

Lord Samuel of Wych Cross was a successful businessman who transformed Land Securities Investment Trust from a small business into Land Securities plc, a leading property development company that played a major role in reshaping London's appearance in the second half of the twentieth century. In 1951 he bought his first painting from Edward Speelman, an eminent dealer and expert in Old Master paintings, and over the next few decades went on to build one of the most important collections of seventeenth-century Low Countries paintings in Britain. Only thirteen were purchased at auction, with many acquired from two private collections. Buying for personal pleasure and to hang in his home, Lord Samuel, a modest and private individual, rarely opened his collection to experts and museum professionals.

Intending it to remain intact and to be seen in the appropriate context of a house, rather than a museum or gallery, after his death in 1987 the City of London Corporation discovered that Lord Samuel had bequeathed his pictures for permanent display in the Mansion House, the official residence of the Lord Mayor. The Corporation were further indebted to Lady Samuel for her decision to convey the pictures to the City immediately, rather than retaining them for her lifetime, as Lord Samuel bequeathed.

The pragmatic, self-interested Dutch valued well-crafted pictures that reflected their own world back to them; however, many pictures also contain allusions, symbols or references giving them deeper meaning. With the Netherlands enjoying economic prosperity, many people could afford to buy oil paintings. The importance of art and the demand for pictures meant that in mid-seventeenth-century Amsterdam there were twice as many registered painters as there were bakers, and three times more than there were butchers. Artists' individual styles varied greatly. A particularly detailed handling of oil paint was possible on copper panel, readily available from coppersmiths because of the demand for engraving plates; of the works in the collection, fifteen are on copper supports, seventeen are on canvas and fifty-two are on oak panels.

Ruisdael visited Bentheim Castle in Westphalia around 1650, when he travelled to the German border on a sketching trip with his friend Claes Berchem. He went on to incorporate the castle into at least fourteen paintings, done throughout his career, depicting it from many different angles, elevations and points of view. None is topographically accurate; in reality the castle has a more modest appearance, set on a low rise in relatively flat countryside. It has been assumed that in emphasising its imposing grandeur Ruisdael's intentions were symbolic; he had a fascination with castles and watchtowers on mountain tops. In this version a low viewpoint dramatises the steepness of the wooded hillside and the size of the castle,

(continues on next page)

◀ Jacob Isaacksz van Ruisdael,
The Castle of Bentheim
Oil on canvas, *c.* 1655
GAG 3758

◀ Frans Hals, *The Merry Lute Player*
Oil on panel, *c.* 1624–28
GAG 3725

▶ Nicolaes Maes, *A Young Woman Sewing*
Oil on panel, 1655
GAG 3736

(continued from previous page)

which looms above the tiny and insignificant travellers on the path below; the sky is threatening and dark.

The Merry Lute Player made headline news when it was bought for Lord Samuel at a New York auction in 1963, partly for its record price but mostly because this was the first occasion on which the bidding was conducted by telephone from London. This lively painting is one of a group that Hals painted in the mid-1620s of life-size, half-length figures drinking or making music and wearing fanciful or theatrical costume. Hals was interested in amateur drama and was a member of the Haarlem rhetoricians' chamber. The instrument seems to be a tenor seven-course lute with a body formed of alternating light and dark wood.

Nicolaes Maes spent most of his artistic career in Amsterdam and is best known for small-scale household interiors such as that of the young seamstress shown here. His subjects often exemplify quiet, patient goodness; spinning, sewing and lacemaking were activities traditionally associated with domestic virtue in women. The painting was acquired by Samuel from Speelman in 1967. **JJ**

Robert Hooke and Restoration science

For nearly three hundred years Robert Hooke was the forgotten man of English science, eclipsed by brighter stars such as Sir Isaac Newton and Sir Christopher Wren, but more recently his achievements have come to be better recognised. He is remembered for Hooke's Law, the theory of elasticity familiar from school physics, but that is only one of his many contributions to knowledge. Hooke was a major scientific figure, publishing the first fully (and beautifully) illustrated scientific textbook, *Micrographia* (1665), which introduced the microscope as an indispensible instrument and showed the wonders of cellular structure. Samuel Pepys recorded in his diary his fascination with this book, sitting up late reading it and wondering at the fantastic illustrations. Hooke experimented widely and invented many devices, including the spring balance (which he sketched in his diary).

Born on the Isle of Wight in 1635, Hooke studied at Oxford before moving to London in the early 1660s. Shortly afterwards he became curator to the Royal Society and Gresham Professor of Geometry and was hired by the City Corporation as a surveyor and architect. Working with Wren after the Great Fire in 1666, he was closely involved in the design of many buildings and new street layouts, including Bethlehem Hospital (Bedlam), the Monument, the Royal College of Physicians and numerous City churches.

Hooke's contribution to science and architecture is clearly revealed in his diary, purchased by the Corporation in 1891, along with some other papers of his, as part of the sale of Moor Hall, Harlow. They had previously been preserved by George Scott (1708–1780), an antiquary and Fellow of the Royal Society. The diary runs from 10 March 1672 to 16 May 1683, and shows Hooke's scientific thoughts and experiments rubbing up against his work as City Surveyor. The diary also describes his evenings out in City taverns and coffee houses, his diet, his physical symptoms and mental states and the (experimental and dangerous) medicines/drugs he took. He had a spine deformity and suffered from a series of minor ailments, which may have contributed to his reputation for irascibility.

Unlike his published work and unlike Pepys's diary, Hooke's diary is not an easy read. It is the memorandum book of a secretive man in a perpetual hurry. Hooke's use of symbols in the diary is evidence of his drive to express science in a more rational and internationally understandable way but also of his haste and secrecy (his private life is hidden from immediate view – again, unlike Pepys – by the use of a symbol to denote sexual intercourse). The diary has been used extensively in recent years as a major source for the biographies and other works celebrating the tercentenary of Hooke's death in 1703. **CT**

▲ ▼ ▶ **Robert Hooke, Diary** (details)
Manuscript on paper, 1672–83
LMA CLC/495/MS01758

Sunday. bought further of springs & mapps. DH. Grace & Mary at Kelly w:th Crawley at Jonathans.

Munday Aug: 5. Directed m:r Crawley for cleaning 3 year clock. to moses Pitts dined there w:th Lloyd wren Pett about Allas...

...Scarborough Received for me from y:e chamber y:e 40:l for w:ch I had a ticket from S:r Chr: Wren July the 13:th last post. Seale I have not lost it.

Tuesday. w:th Pitt to D:r Lloyd. talked w:th him farther at coffe house. walked w:th y:e Secretary to S:t James told him of mapps of making...

...at Jonathans. Lamb &c. at 10 pp. m:r Pitt gave me a bond to pay me 200:l at michaelmas next upon which...

...Wensday at Bloomsbery. w:th Hoskins. then to D:r montacues. he desired Iohane Marriage Railes done. to y:e Secretarys. he told me of...

...moorelands barometer. talkd w:th Charles Kellereway. him at Lady Harvey. and At Dean Lloyd told him my continuance...

Thursd. at home writing minutes of two last thursdays till dutch man call me to Pr: Rupert. at S:r Chr: Wren Cartwright ended...

...S:r C Wren & Oliver. At Garraways w:th m:r Henshaw. told him my Idea of mapps. and about weather clock. DH...

...gave me introduction to y:e Kiopick history. hot meeting to Wed: Hodder Aubrey Haak then in Parlor. D:r Hodder told...

...virtue of Horehound in expelling poyson by being any way taken inwardly or applyed outwardly...

At Jonathans. Lamb. Lodowick &c.

...wrote notes of y:e 29 of July. Cranier & another Dutchman here. DH continued about maps. at S:r J Moors saw his maps...

Sat. 10. Rd a note from Tillotson to Direct masons at Pauls. His Bishop of London kindness...

At Jonathans w:th Colwall & croon all y:e afternoon at m:r Ashmoles much...

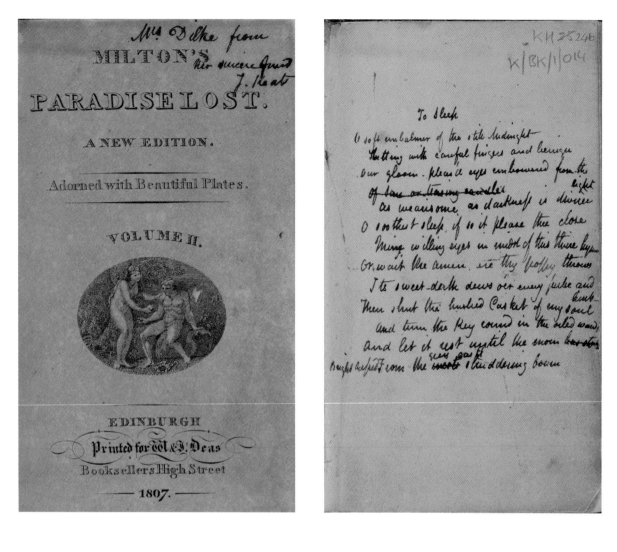

John Keats

Keats House in Hampstead is the last English residence of the poet John Keats, where he lived from 1818 to 1820, before he went to Rome to seek relief from the tuberculosis of which he soon afterwards died. It was built in 1814–16, originally as two houses: Keats lived in one and his girl next door, Fanny Brawne, in the other (they were engaged but never married). The house has been run as a museum since the 1920s, and in 1997 the City Corporation took it over, as Keats was born in the City and had strong roots there. The associated collections include some poignant artefacts, such as Keats's death mask and Fanny's engagement ring, and also some important Keats letters and other documentary items.

Keats's copy of Milton's *Paradise Lost* would be a desirable book as it is, but it is made additionally special by the presence of his annotations, and a draft, written on the flyleaf, of his sonnet 'To Sleep' ('O soft embalmer of the still midnight / Shutting with careful fingers and benign / Our gloom-pleas'd eyes …'). This was probably written at Hampstead in April 1819 and is closely related to his 'Ode to Psyche' and 'Ode to a Nightingale', both written around the same time. Keats probably gave the volumes to Maria Dilke, the wife of the original occupant of one half of the house, when he left for Italy in September 1820; the second volume has the title page inscribed 'Mrs Dilke from her sincere friend J. Keats'.

The Keats House collection includes fifteen autograph letters by Keats to his family and friends, including two written to Fanny Brawne in 1820 after the onset of his illness. One of these (shown opposite) was sold at auction in London in March 2011 and acquired for the house where it was written, with the help of the Heritage Lottery Fund and others. It is as poignant as it is brief; confined to his bed after suffering lung haemorrhages that marked the onset of tuberculosis, Keats wrote of kissing a ring that Fanny had given him, and the frustration of being kept from her: 'I shall Kiss your name and mine where your Lips have been – Lips! why should a poor prisoner as I am talk about such things. … I will be as obstinate as a Robin, I will not sing in a cage – Health is my expected heaven.' At the end he wrote, 'You had better not come to day.' His condition rallied a little thereafter but relapsed in June; in September 1820 he left for Rome, where he died the following February. **MS, KP**

▶ **John Keats, letter to Fanny Brawne**
Manuscript on paper, late February/early March 1820
KH K/MS/02/222

Miss Brawne

You had better not come to day

My dearest Fanny,

The power of your benediction is of not so weak a nature as to pass from the ring in four and twenty hours. it is like a sacred Chalice once consecrated and ever consecrate. I shall kiss your name and mine where your Lips have been - Lips! why should a poor prisoner as I am talk about such things. Thank God, though I hold them the dearest pleasures in the universe, I have a consolation independent of them in the certainty of your affection. I could write a song in the style of Tom Moore's Pathetic about Memory if that would be any relief to me. No. It would not. I will be as obstinate as a Robin, I will not sing in a cage. Health is my expected heaven and you are the Houri - this word I believe is both singular and plural - if only plural, never mind - You are a thousand of them.

Ever yours affectionately
my dearest - J.K.

▲ **Gold ring, set with an almandine stone, given to Fanny Brawne by John Keats, *c.* 1820**
KH K/AR/01/018

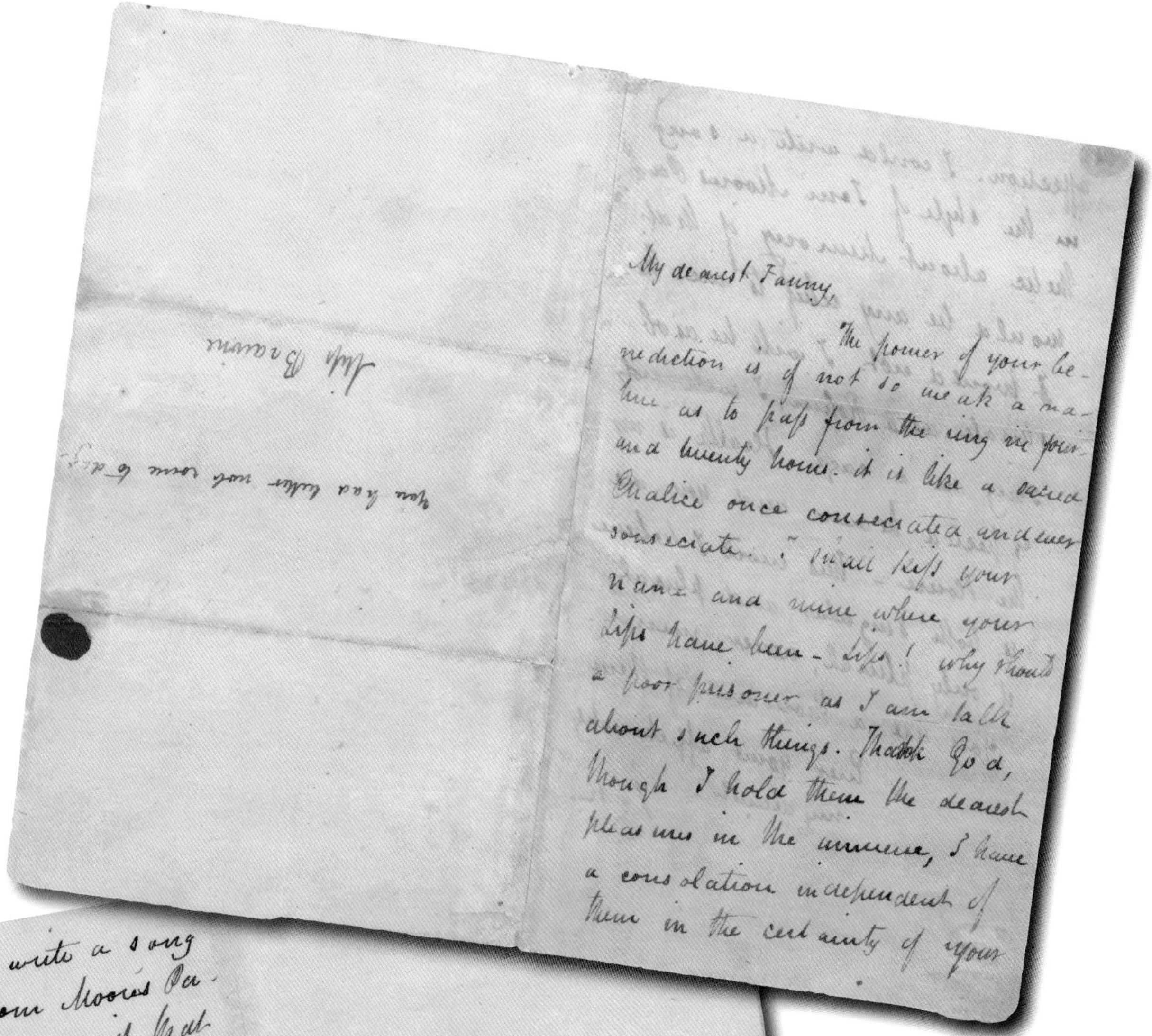

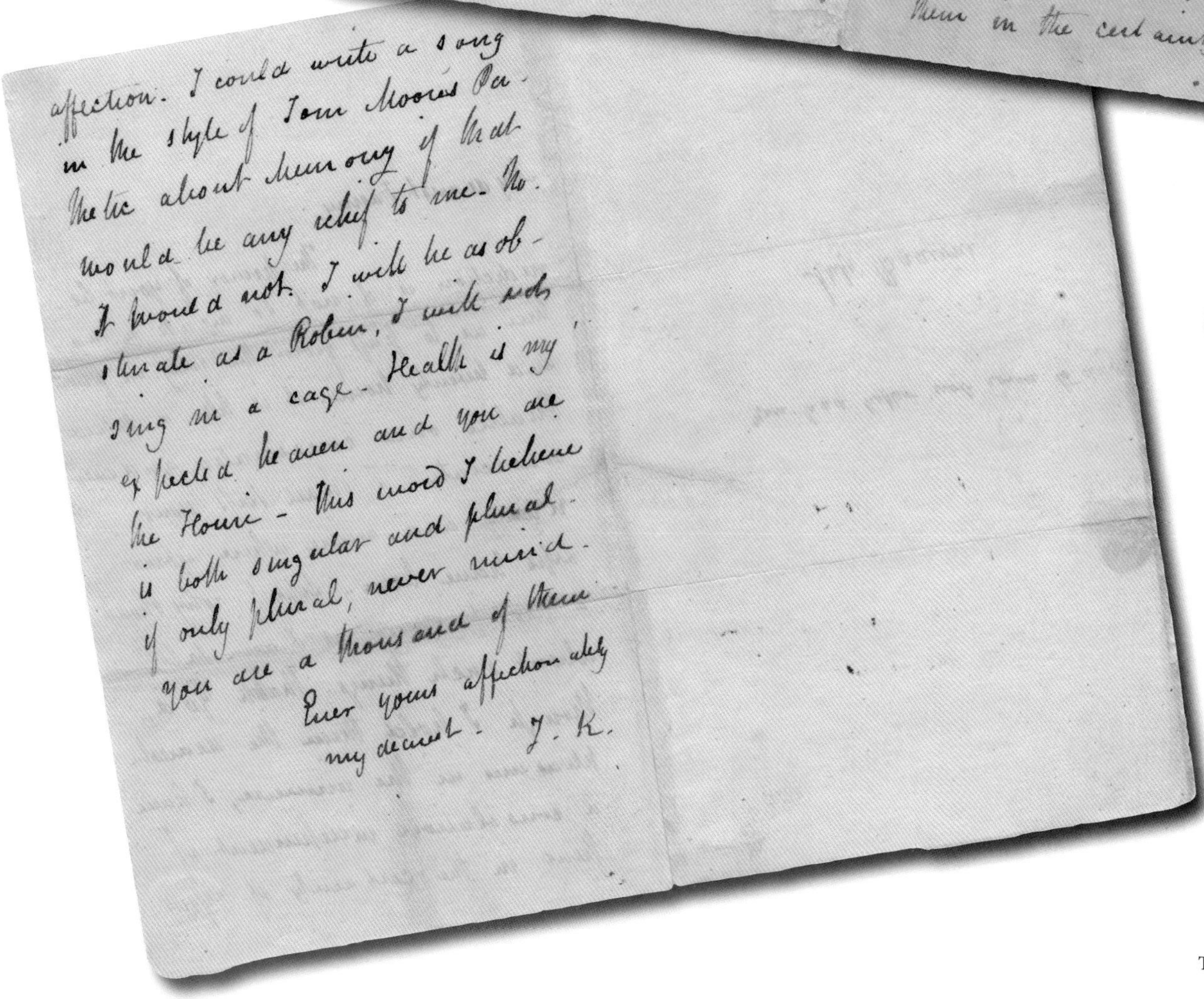

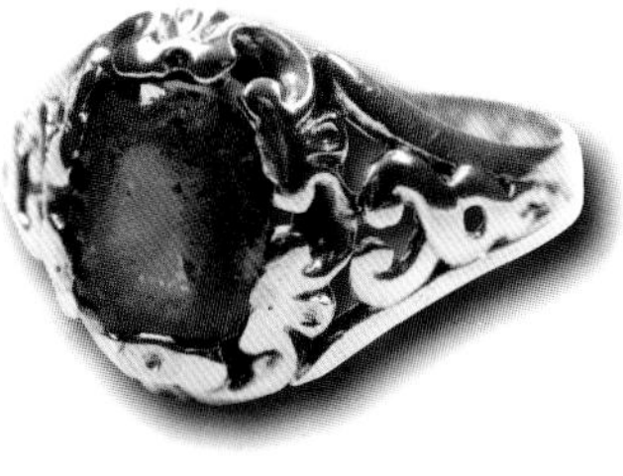

Artists in trouble

The records of judicial proceedings provide us with many stories, some sad and lamentable, others scandalous and disturbing. One feature of these collections that never fails to capture the popular imagination is the plight of artists or celebrities of the day who found themselves on the wrong side of the law.

Ben Jonson (depicted, right) was twenty-six when he was indicted for manslaughter at the Middlesex Sessions of the Peace. A young actor and playwright, he had worked with the Admiral's Men at The Rose since 1597. By the summer of 1598 it seems likely that he had already written several unrecorded plays for the company as well as *Every Man in his Humour* and the infamous *Isle of Dogs*, co-written with Thomas Nashe. The piece was deemed offensive enough to be suppressed, and Jonson served a short term in Marshalsea Prison.

In September 1598 he was in trouble again. The indictment that arraigned him to appear at the October jail delivery session records that on 22 September in the fields at Shoreditch he killed Gabriel Spencer after inflicting a mortal wound to his right side with a rapier. Spencer was a fellow actor, and the injury was the result of a duel. Jonson admitted the crime but was able to use his literary background to save himself. He pleaded for benefit of clergy, a legal loophole that since the twelfth century had placed clergymen and others who could read outside the jurisdiction of the secular courts. By passing a literacy test (usually by reading Psalm 51, commonly known as the 'neck verse'), Jonson escaped the noose but was branded on the thumb with the 'Tyburn T', a mark that disqualified him from making the plea again.

▲ Middlesex Sessions of the Peace, sessions roll, jail delivery, Ben Jonson
Manuscript on vellum, 1598
LMA MJ/SR/0358/068

◄ Portrait of Ben Jonson
Stipple engraving on paper, 1863
LMA SC/GL/NOB/C/078/22

Another great name of literature, Oscar Wilde, is found among the inmates listed in the 1895 register of Wandsworth Prison. Wilde had been sentenced to two years' hard labour along with his alleged lover Alfred Taylor following a very public trial. The Marquess of Queensberry, incensed by Wilde's relationship with his son, publicly slandered Wilde as a 'posing sodomite'. Wilde subsequently took Queensberry to court on a charge of libel but lost the case and quickly found himself up on charges of both sodomy and gross indecency. Conviction led to a sentence of two years in Wandsworth Prison. The register lists him by his full name (Oscar Fingal O'Flaherty Wills Wilde), with the occupation 'author'. His incarceration was the beginning of a personal decline that ended in illness and his death in Paris just five years later, aged forty-six.

The papers of the Middlesex Sessions of the Peace record that Leigh Hunt, critic, essayist, writer and friend of Keats and Shelley, was also sentenced to two years' imprisonment. In 1813 Hunt was the editor of his brother John's newspaper *The Examiner*. They published a criticism of the Prince Regent which led to a charge of libel and an appearance at the Old Bailey in February 1813. According to proceedings published in the *Newgate Calendar*, the affidavit prepared by the Hunt brothers was dismissed by Mr Justice LeBlanc, who stated that the head of the country was not to be 'held up in public newspapers, in the manner you have held up the Prince Regent, as an object of detestation and abhorrence'. The brothers were ordered to pay a fine of £500 each and were separately imprisoned, John in Cold Bath Fields and Leigh in the Surrey County Gaol in Southwark. Given that a further £500 each was required in security and a surety of £250 was to be payable by the brothers on release in lieu of good behaviour for the next five years, it turned out to be a very costly criticism. However, Leigh Hunt continued to write during his period of incarceration, and the court records even include a petition (right) from his brother for paper and pens. **LW**

Dickens in the City

An archive's exterior will often provide no clue that concealed in its pages are renowned names from history. The City Corporation's collections include numerous traces of the career of Charles Dickens (depicted far right), who turns up in a range of archives highlighting aspects of his intimate relationship with London.

Dickens held several occupations before becoming a famous novelist. With the help of a distant relative he became a freelance court reporter, based at the ecclesiastical court known as Doctors' Commons. In *David Copperfield* Dickens describes life there as a 'cosey, dosey, old-fashioned, time-forgotten, sleepy-headed little family party'. The court was also parodied in *Sketches by Boz*, *Nicholas Nickleby* and *Bleak House*. The deposition shown here is an example of the kind of document that Dickens spent his time writing up before escaping into a journalistic and literary career.

Soon after his time as a court reporter, Dickens became a distinguished journalist for the newspaper *The Morning Chronicle*. His social circle broadened to include other journalists, such as the eventual editor of *The Evening Chronicle*, George Hogarth. Dickens became close friends of the Hogarth family and eventually fell in love with George's daughter Catherine. Charles and 'Kate' were soon married, and the wedding took place at St Luke's, Chelsea, where it was duly recorded in the parish register. They had ten children together before separating in 1858.

As a child himself, Dickens laboured in a miserable boot-blacking factory. This early experience, coupled with the appalling conditions of the Victorian workhouse, influenced works such as *Oliver Twist*. Years later Dickens became heavily involved in charity work in a bid to improve social conditions, particularly for women and children. He helped establish a women's home (Urania Cottage), developed support for the ragged school movement (which created free charity schools for poor children) and often visited workhouses and institutions. Although known as a critic of the workhouse and of the Poor Law Amendment Act of 1834, Dickens approved of progress where he found it. For instance, in 1863 he visited the Limehouse Children's Establishment: 'I have never visited any similar establishment, with so much pleasure', he wrote. 'I have never seen any so well administered, and I have never seen children more reasonably, humanely and intelligently treated.' **JG**

▲ Copy depositions from London Consistory Court, in the hand of Charles Dickens
Manuscript on paper, 1830
LMA P69/BAT3/B/064/MS20778

◀ St Luke's, Chelsea, marriage register (entry for Charles Dickens's marriage)
Manuscript and print on paper, 1835–37, fol. 67
LMA P74/LUK/208

I have never visited any similar establishment, with so much pleasure. I have never seen any so well administered and I have never seen children more reasonably, humanely, and intelligently treated.

Charles Dickens

Wednesday Twenty Seventh May, 1863.

This establishment seems to produce better results — so far as they can be judged at a single visit — than any I have ever inspected. — and I have been over many pauper schools.

W H Wills.

27th May 1863

I continue to observe progress in improvement at each visit. in the naval drill especially

Edwin Chadwick

I have great pleasure in adding my testimony to the admirable efficiency of this establishment which is the best of its kind I have ever visited. —

J N Woodgate &c.

29 May 1863 I have examined the whole of this establishment during three days, and am glad to record the same favourable opinion of its management, which I have expressed after former inspections. The treatment of the children is more uniformly good & appropriate to their condition, & withal more economical than in any similar school that I am acquainted with

E C Tufnell

◀ Stepney Board of Guardians, Limehouse Children's Establishment visitors' book
Manuscript on paper, 1850–71, fol. 30
LMA STBG/L/122/001

▲ Portrait of Charles Dickens
Stipple engraving on paper, c. 1860
LMA SC/GL/NOB/C/078/22

Pre-Raphaelite treasures

The Pre-Raphaelite paintings in Guildhall Art Gallery are among its best-known treasures. Many were acquired through the efforts of Alfred Temple, the gallery's first director, who persuaded Charles Gassiot, a successful City wine merchant, to bequeath his collection to the City Corporation in 1902. Some, however, were acquired by Temple himself, who bought *The Eve of St Agnes* for the gallery from his own pocket but was subsequently reimbursed.

This painting illustrates an episode from Keats's famous poem, when Madeline and her lover, Porphyro, escape from her father's house during the festivities on St Agnes' Eve. William Holman Hunt, the artist, discovered this poem in 1847 and felt it expressed 'the sacredness of honest responsible love and the weakness of proud intemperance'. When the picture appeared at the 1848 Royal Academy exhibition, it attracted the attention of Dante Gabriel Rossetti, who came up and introduced himself to Hunt. Hunt, Rossetti and John Everett Millais became the three principal members of the Pre-Raphaelite Brotherhood, founded in opposition to what seemed to them to be the Academy's stuffy ideals and outworn teaching methods.

For *My First Sermon* Millais used his daughter Effie as a model, sitting in one of the old high-backed pews in All Saints Church, Kingston upon Thames. It was an immediate success, and the Archbishop of Canterbury, during a speech at the Royal Academy in May 1863, introduced it with the words 'We should feel the happier by the touching representations of playfulness, the innocence, and [...] the piety of childhood.' It was so popular that Millais painted a companion picture in the following year, *My Second Sermon*, showing the same child asleep: the novelty of ecclesiastical oratory had worn off.

Rossetti is most famously represented in the gallery's collections with *La Ghirlandata* (reproduced p. 8). This was painted while he was staying at Kelmscott Manor, the Oxfordshire house he part-owned with his friend William Morris, following his breakdown and suicide attempt in 1872. Although Morris stayed away, his daughters and his wife, Jane (with whom Rossetti was in love), were there. The honeysuckle and roses around the top of the harp in this picture indicate sexual attraction, while the harp itself represents music, a common metaphor for love and lovemaking. The model for the picture was not Jane Morris but Alexa Wilding, 'a really good-natured creature', who became one of Rossetti's most frequent models. The intense use of colour creates a brooding, melancholy mood. JJ

▲ William Holman Hunt,
The Eve of St Agnes (The Flight of Madeline and Porphyro during the Drunkeness attending the Revelry)
Oil on canvas, 1848
GAG 1033

▶ Sir John Everett Millais,
My First Sermon
Oil on canvas, 1863
GAG 701

The Sir Matthew Smith Collection

Matthew Smith, knighted in 1954, towards the end of his life, was a highly successful British artist of the first half of the twentieth century, whose bold colours and distinctive style led Augustus John to describe him as 'one of the most brilliant and individual figures in modern British painting'. Francis Bacon, who was influenced by Smith, referred to his use of paint as 'a direct assault upon the nervous system'. An extensive collection of Smith's paintings is one of the particular strengths of the modern holdings of Guildhall Art Gallery.

Smith was born in Halifax in 1879 and struggled against family resistance to be allowed to realise his aspiration to become an artist. He studied at the Slade School in London for a while, but it was in France that his vocation began to blossom. His lifelong association with and love for that country began in 1908, when he moved to an artists' colony in Pont-Aven in Brittany; he later said that in France 'my life began: my mind began to open out'. After the First World War Smith continued to cross between London and France for the next twenty years, painting the women who were important to him (particularly Madame Monay, the wife of the artist Pierre Monay, and Christiane de Mauberge) as well as landscapes in the south of France and still-life subjects.

In November 1934 Smith moved into the Hotel le Cagnard at Cagnes-sur-Mer, where he remained until February 1936. The proprietress's daughter was Christiane de Mauberge, described by Smith as 'demie Raphael, demie Gauguin' ('half-Raphael, half-Gauguin'), and she was the model for all his figure paintings of this period. Christiane later recalled that he would paint in a frenzy and, on finishing, break an egg into a glass, down it and throw himself utterly exhausted on to a sofa. Their relationship was circumscribed by her religious faith and Smith's married status, and during the war Christiane became a nun. This painting, dated 1936 on the reverse, was probably begun somewhat earlier, possibly in 1934.

Smith died in 1959. His studio collection came to the Guildhall Art Gallery in 1974, when his heir, his friend and model Mary Keene, presented 175 oil paintings and over a thousand watercolours and drawings to the City Corporation. At that time Guildhall Art Gallery had yet to be rebuilt, and Mrs Keene was excited by the plans for the new art gallery in the Barbican Centre. Following the Barbican's important Smith exhibition in 1983, Barbican Art Gallery displayed changing selections from the collection from 1984 to 2000, while curatorial responsibility remained with Guildhall Art Gallery. Subsequently, following the rebuilding there, the paintings were transferred to Guildhall, with the gallery taking on the responsibility of exhibiting changing displays from the collection on a permanent basis. **JJ**

◄ Sir Matthew Smith, *Lady with a Rose* (portrait of Christiane de Mauberge)
Oil on canvas, *c.* 1934–36
GAG 2027

Mrs. Peter

Could it be that we're getting a bit frenzied in our search for ways of ~~assuaging our~~ ~~creative urges~~ using ready made foods and at the same time assuaging our creative urges in the kitchen? When it comes to buying a swiss roll, unrolling it, ~~re-spreading~~ scraping off the filling and ~~replacing~~ it with a broken down brick of bought ice cream I can't help wondering. The advice, given it is true, as an alternative to making your own Swiss roll, comes in ~~but~~ Cooking with Can & Pack by Fanny & Johnnie Cradock...

Food, wine and the Elizabeth David Collection

Guildhall Library holds a number of important collections on food and wine, mostly acquired during the twentieth century. The André Simon Collection is based on the personal library of the eminent food writer and historian of that name (1877–1970), who used Guildhall Library extensively in the early 1900s, when writing the first of his many books. The Institute of Masters of Wine have also deposited their library, including the books of the Wine Trade Club and others, at Guildhall. This has over two thousand volumes, from the seventeenth century to the present day, relating to the making, selling and consuming of wine, and is one of the best collections in the field in a public institution.

Elizabeth David (1913–1992) is regarded by many as one of the most influential food writers of the twentieth century and by some as the person who single-handedly dragged British food out of the doldrums of a ration-wracked 1950s. Later in life, as her writing became increasingly scholarly, she carried out much of her extensive research at Guildhall Library, and following her death in 1992 the City acquired 900 books from David's personal collection. In cataloguing them it was discovered that many of these books had arrived with David's notes, jottings and autograph manuscripts tucked inside.

In person David could be fearsomely direct and opinionated, and although this was not generally reflected in her writing, in the unpublished review illustrated here we can see something of her struggle between remaining professional and expressing her true opinions. The review is of Fanny and Johnnie Cradock's *Cooking with Can & Pack* (1961), a collection of short-cut recipes using canned, frozen and other convenience foods. It is hard to imagine two more different food writers; Fanny Cradock was all show and bluster, presenting over-decorated, pseudo-French food in an extrovert manner on many TV programmes. In contrast, David, a very private person who managed to avoid the television cameras until towards the end of her life, was never concerned about dressing up her food, but only about authenticity and flavour.

David's strikethroughs have left her original thoughts still legible as she tested how far she could go in showing up the Cradocks' combination of penny-pinching and pretension. 'Could it be that we're getting a bit frenzied in our search for ways of using ready made foods and at the same time assuaging our creative urges in the kitchen? When it comes to buying a swiss roll, unrolling it, scraping off the filling and re-spreading it with a broken down brick of bought ice cream I can't help wondering.' At one point she suggests that they have carried what was essentially a sound idea 'to the point of dementia'. But the Cradocks fared better than the ladies of the Belfast Women's Institute Club, whose 1945 pamphlet on *Ulster Fare* – coping, admittedly, with the trials of wartime rationing – prompted David's marginal annotation 'the most revolting dish ever devised' for an 'Italian salad' combining macaroni, tinned pears and minced onions. **PR**

Publishers' archives

The archives of publishers provide particularly rich seams for literary and cultural historians, as they help to reveal all the processes and decisions that feed into book production and often reveal relationships between authors, illustrators and publishers. London Metropolitan Archives holds collections from a number of mainstream and smaller publishing houses; the archives of Bogle-L'Ouverture Publications are described earlier (see p. 96), while the illustrations here come from the archive of Hodder & Stoughton.

This firm, established in 1868, was for many years the leading British publisher of popular fiction, especially through its famous Yellow Jacket series. It had an exceptionally strong religious list (originally the backbone of its business) and was a significant publisher of scientific, exploration and technical publications. It also published two highly influential periodicals, *The Bookman* and *The British Weekly*. Its position as a major publisher, as demonstrated by its archives, continued throughout the twentieth century. In 1993 Hodder & Stoughton Ltd merged with Headline Book Publishing to become Hodder Headline plc.

This substantial collection provides much information about the multifaceted business of publishing. Of notable importance are the forty-six authors' ledgers, 1907–61, supplemented by publishing and other ledgers, 1886–1968. These are further supported by considerable quantities of other material, such as company minutes, sales reports, publicity material, and a number of author files, 1939–93. The archive contains much about the company's premises, including photographs of bomb damage in the Paternoster Row and Warwick Square area of the City of London in the Second World War. There is also material about the firm's employees, including registers and salary books, staff handbooks and newsletters, and material about company sports days, much of it pictorial.

The records of the subsidiaries and associated companies, such as Edward Arnold Ltd and the Brockhampton Press, sometimes form distinct series, but are often mixed with those of the parent company. The records also include some Hodder family documents (from 1825) and some papers of the Publishers' Association. Finally, the archive includes the private correspondence of Sir Ernest Hodder-Williams (chairman of Hodder and Stoughton, 1902–27), and the papers of the last Chairman of the company, Philip Attenborough, who played a major role in safeguarding the future of the archive.

The archive contains much graphic material, including a scrapbook of plates from books published by Hodder & Stoughton in the first half of the twentieth century. Many of the plates are illustrations by the French-born artist Edmund Dulac, one of the 'Golden Age' illustrators, who had a close association with Hodder & Stoughton through an arrangement with the Leicester Gallery. The gallery would commission paintings from Dulac and then sell the rights to Hodder & Stoughton, who would publish the books (one book a year over many years) while the gallery sold the paintings. **PS**

▶ Edmund Dulac, *Sinbad the Sailor*
and Other Stories (Hodder & Stoughton)
1907
Colour plates of watercolour paintings
LMA CLC/B/119/MS36510

155

▲ Volumes from the shelves at
London Metropolitan Archives

FURTHER READING

There is a huge literature on the history of the City, and
of London. The following is a brief, selective list of places to
start to find out more.

Peter Ackroyd: *London: The Biography*. London, 2000.

Sir John Baddeley: *The Guildhall of the City of London*.
8th edn. London, 1952.

Caroline Barron: *The Medieval Guildhall of London*.
London, 1974.

Simon Bradley and Nikolaus Pevsner: *London: 1, City of
London*. (Buildings of England series) New edn.
New Haven and London, 2002.

Christopher Brooke: *London, 800–1216: The Shaping of
a City*. London, 1975.

*The Corporation of London: Its Origin, Constitution, Powers
and Duties*. London, 1950.

Henry Harben: *A Dictionary of London*. London, 1918.

Tracey Hill: *Pageantry and Power: a Cultural History of the
early Lord Mayor's Show*. Manchester, 2010.

Valerie Hope: *My Lord Mayor: Eight Hundred Years of
London's Mayoralty*. London, 1989.

Nicholas Kenyon (ed.): *The City of London: Architectural
Tradition and Innovation in the Square Mile*. London,
2011.

David Kynaston: *A World of its Own, 1815–1890*; *Golden
Years, 1890–1914*; *Illusions of Gold, 1914–1945*; *A Club no
More, 1945–2000*. 4 vols (The City of London series).
London, 1994–2001.

Roy Porter: *London: A Social History*. London, 1994.

John Stow (ed. H. Wheatley and V. Pearl): *The Survey of
London*. London, 1956.

Ben Weinreb and others: *The London Encyclopedia*. 3rd edn.
London, 2008.

For further details of the City of London Corporation's
collections, see the catalogues and information about the
services by following the links on the City's website:
www.cityoflondon.gov.uk.

INDEX

Page numbers in *italics* are for illustrations

© Scala Publishers Ltd, 2011
Text © City of London Corporation, 2011
Photography © City of London Corporation, 2011

Scala Publishers Ltd
Northburgh House
10 Northburgh Street
London EC1V 0AT
www.scalapublishers.com

Hardback ISBN 978-1-85759-699-1
Paperback ISBN 978-1-85759-740-0

Project editor: Esme West
Copy editor: Matthew Taylor
Proofreader: Julie Pickard
Designer: Yvonne Dedman
Printed and bound in Malaysia

10 9 8 7 6 5 4 3 2 1

British Library Cataloguing in Publication Data
A catalogue record for this book is available from the British Library

LIST OF CONTRIBUTORS

Andrew Harper (AH), Bridget Howlett (BH), Claire Titley (ClT), Charlotte Shaw (CS), Charlie Turpie (CT), Daniel Beagles (DB), David Pearson (DP), David Baldwin (DAB), Elizabeth Scudder (ES), Geoff Pick (GP), Howard Doble (HD), Jeff Gerhardt (JG), Jeremy Johnson (JJ), Jeremy Smith (JS), Jo-Ann Vietzke (JV), Jo Wisdom (JW), Katie Keys (KK), Ken Page (KP), Kevin Sheahan (KS), Laurence Ward (LW), Laura Taylor (LT), Michael Melia (MM), Matthew Payne (MP), Maureen Roberts (MR), Mick Scott (MS), Naomi Allen (NA), Nicola Avery (NiA), Peter Ross (PR), Philippa Smith (PS), Richard Wiltshire (RW), Sharon Tuff (ST) and Valerie Hart (VH)

▲ Detail of the boss of the State Sword
Mansion House Plate Collection
(see p. 4)

19

Wast Smythfyld

Creple gate

Mor

Aldersgate

h

Nawgat

q

fleete Condit

Ludgat

S Brides

grayes Inn

Leicester howse

The temple

Whyt friers

Bryde wel

Black friers

Edwardes castle

Paules wharfe

Broken wharfe

Quene hvthe

Three

T H A M Y

Banckes syde

ambeth

mersh

The Beare howse